The Use of
Magical Oils
in Hoodoo, Prayer, and
Spellwork

GREGORY WHITE

White Willow Books

ISBN: 0692875956
ISBN-13: 978-0692875957

DEDICATION

This book is dedicated to all the rootworkers and conjure doctors that came before me and the ones I practice alongside today.

OTHER BOOKS BY GREGORY WHITE

CLUCKED – The Tale of Pickin Chicken

MAKING SOAP FROM SCRATCH: How to Make
Handmade Soap – A Beginners Guide and Beyond

ESSENTIAL OILS AND AROMATHERAPY: How to
Use Essential Oils for Beauty, Health, and Spirituality

LITTLE HOUSE SEARCH – A Puzzle Book and Tour of
the Works of Laura Ingalls Wilder

CONTENTS

What is a Magical Oil?   3

What is Hoodoo and Spellwork?   6

Ingredients in Spiritual Oils   8

Herbs, Roots, Minerals   17

Way to Use Magical and Spiritual Oils   29

Hoodoo Oils   36

Saint and Angels Oils   58

Working Magic with Oils in Spells, Rituals,   79
and Prayers

Candle Color Associations   82

Spells with Magical Oils   83

Epilogue   106

RESOURCES

All the oils mentioned in this book can be found in our
Nashville, TN retail store as well as our websites at:

www.conjureshop.com

and

www.aromagregory.com

The illustrations found in this book come from a variety of vintage catalogs and other works of art that are now in the public domain. The artist's names have long been forgotten but their talents live on.

Cover art: an 18th century colored engraving titled:
The Wife of an Apothecary

WHAT IS A MAGICAL OIL?

Oils, potions, and magical concoctions are found throughout literature and have been used for spiritual purposes since before recorded history. They have been used to anoint Kings and priests, to cleanse sacred objects, to ensure a pregnancy, and to heal wounds and broken hearts.

Most of my experience stems from the Hoodoo tradition where the creation of oils is used for anointing the body, candles, and objects to cleanse or bring about change. My certification in the field of aromatherapy gives me a deeper understanding of the ingredients that go into making a spiritual oil. I not only know the magical use of each essential oil in a blend, but also the aromatherapeutic benefit and the physical reactions it causes to the mind and body.

Not surprisingly, these benefits often cross over from the practical to the magical side with little effort. Let's take lavender, for example. Lavender is often associated with love spells and to bring about peace and a sense of calm. In aromatherapy, it is used for calming and for relaxation. In the chakra system, it is associated with the 7th chakra - the crown chakra where peace and a connection to the universe and God are experienced. In Hoodoo, it is not only used for love but also for creating floor washes that are intended to bring peace into the home. Many Voodoo recipes use lavender for peace, clarity, and psychic blessings. So, whether it is used in aromatherapy, witchcraft, the chakra system, or a folk magic service —

the benefits are the same — to bring about a sense of peace and harmony.

So, what is anointing? What does it mean to be anointed? The New Testament Greek words for "anoint" are chrio, meaning "to smear or rub with oil" and, by association, "to consecrate for office or religious service"; and aleipho, which means "to anoint." Biblically speaking, people were anointed with oil to imply God's blessing or mark that person's calling in life. One was anointed for a special purpose - to be a king, to be a prophet, etc. In Christian religions that use anointing oil, it is understood that the oil alone has no power. Anointing oils are made according to scriptural specifications, taken from the word of God. Therefore, only God can anoint someone for a religious purpose.

Probably the most well-known account of the use of an anointing oil is the biblical story of Samuel and David. Samuel was known as "the Prophet" and had anointed Saul as the first King of Israel. Before a campaign against the Philistines, Saul was waiting for Samuel to arrive and offer sacrifices to seek God's favor. When Samuel didn't appear as soon as he expected, Saul offered these sacrifices himself, assuming the privileges of a priest. When Samuel arrived, he informed Saul, "You have done a foolish thing," using the Hebrew term 'fool' for people who act without regard for God. Samuel denounces Saul, telling him that his descendants will not rule in his place. At a later date, Saul was given another assignment by God, to destroy the Amalekites. Saul, however, failed this second chance given to him by God by disobeying instructions.

The Lord said to Samuel, "How long will you mourn for Saul, since I have rejected him as king over Israel? Fill your horn with oil and be on your way; I am sending you to Jesse of Bethlehem. I have chosen one of his sons to be king."

The story continues with Saul evaluating each of the sons based on their appearance, contemplating which one would make a good king. However, God chose David, the youngest of the sons.

Then the Lord said, "Rise and anoint him; this is the one." So Samuel took the horn of oil and anointed him in the presence of his brothers, and from that day on the Spirit of the Lord came powerfully upon David.

In the Hoodoo tradition, anointing oils are mainly known as "condition oils," as each one is formulated to tackle a particular condition (problem, a state of mind or body) that a person is experiencing. You will usually only find this term in Hoodoo and conjure practices where the oils are used to anoint the body, candles for rituals, and practical spell casting. While, historically, most practitioners of Hoodoo are Christian, the concept of where the power of the oil comes from is slightly different. It is the combination of the correct herbs, flowers, minerals, and curios that come together to create an oil that is capable of magical change. Many bless the oils after they are made or petition God, ancestors, or distinct Saints to bring forth their blessings to complete the process.

In Witchcraft and some Pagan religions, oils are used not only in spellwork but also a celebration. Some use different oils to mark the turning of the Wheel of the Year. In the Spring, flowers are most often used. Summer is a time of green leaves and fruits. In Autumn, the choices are usually spices and barks. Pure plant oils are considered to be a way to connect with the very nature they come from, bringing more power and connection to spells and magical workings. You will notice that in many Pagan and witchcraft traditions, magic is spelled with a 'k' inserted to differentiate from what most consider to be stage magic.

WHAT IS HOODOO AND SPELLWORK?

Hoodoo is a unique form of American folk magic. Before the internet and our widespread access to information and technology, it was mainly found in the South. Even today, its Southern roots hold firm. Its heritage is African magic. When the Africans were brought to America during the Transatlantic slave trade, they brought with them their spirituality, their deities, their strong belief in ancestor worship, and their magical rituals and customs. However, they no longer had access to their homeland plants. This is how Native American herbal medicine made its way into the customs of the Africans. Over time, blacks incorporated some elements of the European culture, such as occultism and mysticism. With these three belief systems combined, time and practice created this unique form of American folk magic.

Hoodoo is often called by other names including rootwork, conjure, and laying tricks. A practitioner is sometimes called a conjureman (or woman), a rootworker, or a two-headed doctor.

The purpose of Hoodoo was to give power to the powerless. It was a way to access the supernatural to improve their circumstances, bringing good fortune and luck in love, money matters, good health, protection, and even gambling. Similar to other types of folk magic, Hoodoo includes the use of herbs, roots, minerals, animal bones, graveyard dirt, the personal possessions of another, and bodily fluids into the practice. As time went on, pharmacies began carrying products that their black customers sought out and began producing goods and oils such as "Money Drawing" and "Love Attracting" as well as candles and incense for "Fast Luck" and others for gambling, protection, and unhexing. As these products grew in popularity, they began finding their way into catalogs and magazines where the merchandise could be purchased through mail order.

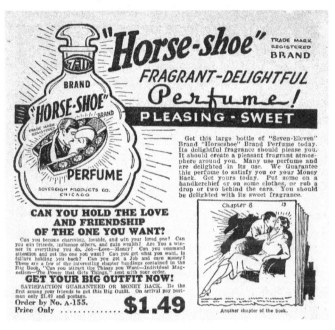

Some have referred to Hoodoo as the "country cousin" of Voodoo or Vodou. The slave owners oppressed the African religions and cultures, insisting the slaves become Christian. As a result, the slaves adopted the Catholic saints into their culture to stand in for their own deities and spirits – usually ones whose domain was the same or similar to their own. Louisiana Voodoo is often confused with Haitian Vodou and Deep Southern Hoodoo. While Louisiana Voodoo is strong among the

Catholic population in Louisiana, most practitioners of Hoodoo have historically (mainly since the 19th century) been Protestant Christians. Moses was seen as the greatest conjureman of all time. That being said, unlike Voodoo, Hoodoo is a system of magic – not a religion. Any religion may practice Hoodoo. With that in mind, most earnest practitioners will tell you that it requires respect for its roots. To leave the African connection out of Hoodoo strongly suggests cultural appropriation.

Spellwork is, quite simply, the crafting of and art of casting spells. It is the direction of energy to manipulate the world around us to create some sort of desired change. This is achieved using metaphysical tools and practices such as the spoken word, herb lore, ritual tools (such as athames and cauldrons), candle magic, and sacred oils. It can either be performed alone (solitary) or within a group of people to form a planned ritual. At the core of it, Hoodoo work is considered spellwork. Spells are performed by many different religions and paths.

THE INGREDIENTS IN SPIRITUAL OILS

Almost all seasoned practitioners of magic will tell you that using all natural ingredients is of utmost importance. Artificial fragrances have no place in serious ritual or spiritual practice because they contain zero life-force. Herbs, roots, and real essential oils carry with them the heart of the plant they come from, its very essence.

This is the very foundation of what is known as 'sympathetic magic.' Sympathetic magic, also known as imitative magic or homeopathic magic, is magic that is based on imitation or correspondence — or both. Imitation is the idea that one thing can represent another thing and, by proxy, stand in its place. The voodoo doll, a poppet, or effigies are examples of imitation magic. For example, a lock of hair or personal item from the intended target will link them to their doll and create a magical bond. It is said that whatever happens to the doll, will also happen to that person. It is the idea that similar actions can create similar results. The rain dance is a form of imitative magic where the dancer is recreating the motions of falling rain to force the rain to fall from the sky.

Correspondence is the other aspect of sympathetic magic and is the one we turn to when using particular herbs, minerals, roots, barks, and flowers in the creation of magical oils. This concept is applied in the use of plants that are considered masculine or feminine. Some phallic-shaped roots are magically used to represent the penis while others, such as Queen Elizabeth root, resemble and are used to symbolize the vagina. The two are often brought together to bring passion back into a relationship or, more simplistically, a male root might be used to treat impotence. In the same way, a female root could be employed in fertility magic for a woman.

This philosophy carries over into the entire magical plant world. When I explain this idea to clients, I always use the rose as an example. Roses symbolize love and are given on special occasions such as Valentine's Day. It is an icon that we all recognize. But, if you were to give your sweetheart stinging nettle or a bag of clove buds, they wouldn't know what to make of it. Neither would be interpreted as an expression of love. So, sympathetically, roses carry love within them. Catnip attracts cats. Therefore it is an herb of attraction and is used in spells to attract things to you. Ancient texts, including the Bible, described the many benefits of Hyssop. In some parts of the world, it had a religious function, and was believed to purify and "forgive sins." Christianity held hyssop in high esteem. The herb was used as a symbol of baptism and reconciliation. It is associated with purification in other religions. It is used for bruising, ear aches, tooth aches, sores, and for calming hysteria. In magical traditions, it is the number one herb used in hex removal. Just as it can holistically expel negatives and pain, it is used the same way magically — to bring the problem to the surface so that it can be expelled or banished.

When we formulate a magical oil using the proper plant ingredients for whatever condition or problem we are facing, we are putting the magic (and ourselves) in direct alignment with the wisdom and inherent knowledge of the plant kingdom. Some would say we are placing ourselves in sympathy with God (or Goddess) and everything he (or she) created.

ABOUT ESSENTIAL OILS - The term "essential oil" is a contraction of the original "quintessential oil." Aristotle presented the idea that matter is made up of four elements: earth, air, fire, and water. The fifth element, or quintessence, was thought to be spirit or life force. Forcing the oils out of a plant was considered to be the process of removing the spirit, or life force, from the plant. Modern knowledge teaches us that essential oils are a delicate balance of naturally occurring chemicals found in plants. Today, most essential oils are extracted by either the distillation process or by using the cold process. The first relies on water and heat to remove the precious oils. The latter, in simple terms, is achieved by pressing or squeezing the oils out — most often used in citrus plants because the oils are found plentiful in the peels. It is an interesting idea that when we blend our magical oils, using essential oils as part of the ingredients, that we are calling upon the spirits inside the plant.

Almost every essential oil has a magical correspondence

to it because they are derived from plants. The main thing to remember is to use real essential oils – not an artificial fragrance. To name all of the magical properties of essential oils could be an entire book on its own. Below is a quick glance of some of the mystical powers associated with essential oils.

- For love and sex, there is sandalwood, ylang-ylang, lavender, patchouli, vanilla, jasmine, just to name a few.

- For happiness, use any of the citrus oils: orange, tangerine, mandarin, and pink grapefruit. The exception would be lemon oil, which you would save for a spell that deals with souring.

- To gain power and success, try oils of bergamot, frankincense, bay rum, or wintergreen.

- In matters of attraction, there are essential oils such as chamomile, geranium, patchouli, anise, and vetiver.

- When finances are strained, and you want to bring in more money try oils of cinnamon, ginger, nutmeg, patchouli, and clary sage.

- For work of a baneful nature, go with hot and the sour oils such as black pepper, cedarwood, lemon, or vandal root.

History tells us the ways aromatic oils were extracted before the perfection of the distillation process. One method, maceration, is very close to the way we create anointing oils today. Plant matter (petals, leaves, stems) are packed into a vessel and covered in a vegetable oil - usually olive oil. The oil was then heated, forcing the essential oils to release into the olive oil. There is a more subtle method that I refer to as 'infused oil' where the plant matter is placed into a glass jar and covered with a carrier oil. It is then left on a sunny windowsill for six to eight weeks and is shaken every day to disperse the plant matter throughout the oil. At the end of the waiting period, the plants are strained out of the oil. Once finished, it isn't actually what is called 'essential oil' but makes for an excellent massage oil or spiritual oil base. This solar method, however, can speed up the process of your carrier oil becoming rancid due to its exposure to heat. I have found that that same effect can be achieved without introducing direct sunlight. Store in a cabinet or other dark area for eight to twelve weeks and shake whenever you remember to (although daily is best.) Strain and bottle the infused oil.

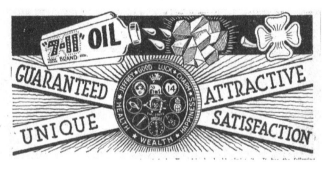

The Egyptians were master perfumers and had extensive knowledge of aromatic compounds and how to use them for beauty, spirituality, and as medicine. Hieroglyphics reveal the recipe for their famous Kyphi incense using a mixture of honey, raisins soaked in wine, frankincense, myrrh, sweet flag, pine resin, and juniper. They used aromatic oils in the mummification process, frankincense being the most widely practiced oil. When King Tutankhamen's tomb was opened in 1922, 50 alabaster jars designed to hold 350 liters of oils were discovered.

The Ebers Papyrus, discovered in 1862 by Edwin Smith, is an Egyptian medical papyrus dating to c. 1550 BCE. Besides including 877 prescriptions, it is full of incantations and concoctions meant to drive away disease-causing demons. The Egyptians favored the method of extracting oil by soaking the plant matter in goose fat, another example of an 'infused oil.'

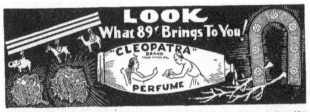

To create a genuine anointing oil, you will need a base oil, also known as a carrier oil, to suspend the herbs and essential oils in. This dilutes the essential oils used to make them safe and mild on the skin. Historically, olive oil was the principal carrier oil used in anointing oils. These days, a wide range of oils are available to us such as sweet almond, grapeseed, avocado, sunflower, castor oil, macadamia nut oil, and the list goes on. Other than olive oil, my two favorite base oils are jojoba or fractionated coconut oil because they both have a long shelf life and resist rancidity. Our own magical oils use a base of fractionated coconut oil. It differs from regular coconut oil, which is solid. The chain of fatty acids has been spun out of the coconut oil, leaving behind only the liquid element. Without the fatty acids present, fractionated coconut oil's shelf life increases dramatically. It also glides across the skin well and is readily absorbed.

HOLY ANOINTING OIL - The recipe for holy anointing oil which was given to Moses by God is found the Bible in Exodus 30:23-24 - Take the finest spices: five hundred shekels of free-flowing myrrh; half that amount, that is, two hundred and fifty shekels, of fragrant cinnamon; two hundred and fifty shekels of fragrant cane; five hundred shekels of cassia—all according to the standard of the sanctuary shekel; together with a hin of olive oil;

Most botanists and religious scholars associate the Biblical fragrant cane with the Acorus calamus variety calamus which gives us the ingredients as myrrh, cinnamon, cassia, calamus, and olive oil. 500 shekels is the equivalent to about 12.5 pounds of material. A hin of olive oil would equal one gallon. Unless you plan on anointing your entire town, I've broken down the recipe to accommodate a smaller and more affordable batch.

This recipe is .5% of the original recipe. Use if you want the blend to be exact according to the Bible:

1 ounce of myrrh essential oil

1 ounce of cassia essential oil

1/2 ounce of cinnamon essential oil

1/2 ounce of calamus essential oil

.64 ounce of olive oil

With that being said, as a certified aromatherapist, I find this blend to be very low in a carrier oil in ratio to the essential oils, which might be considered irritating to the skin. So, if you don't mind stepping away from the pure Biblical recipe, see my revised recipe on the next page.

REVISED HOLY OILS RECIPE

1/2 (15ml) ounce of myrrh essential oil

1/2 (15ml) ounce of cassia essential oil

1/4 (7.5ml) ounce of cinnamon essential oil

1/4 (7.5ml) ounce of calamus essential oil

8 (236.58ml) ounces of olive oil or other carrier oil.

ABRAMELIN OIL - The oil is described in The Book of Abramelin by Abraham of Worms, a Jew from Worms, Germany. While no records can confirm it, he is said to have lived from c.1362–c.1458. The Book of Abramelin tells of an Egyptian mage named Abraham who taught a magical system to Abraham Worms. The system of magic from this book found new popularity in the 19th and 20th centuries thanks to Samuel Liddell MacGregor Mathers who translated the book and retitled it, The Book of the Sacred Magic of Abramelin the Mage. Mathers, a British occultist, and Freemason integrated these teachings into the Hermetic Order of the Golden Dawn, an organization devoted to the study and practice of the occult, metaphysics, and paranormal. They were considered a magical order that studied astrology, geomancy, Tarot divination, and scrying. Their rituals and practices helped to form the magical roots of what is now known as Wicca and Thelema. As far as the recipe for this oil goes, Mathers took it upon himself to alter the original recipe that was recorded by Worms. The original recipe is the same as the holy oil given to Moses by God, as told in the Bible: myrrh, cassia, cinnamon, calamus, and olive oil. Mathers switched out the ingredient calamus for galangal root. Some say this is a translation error. Others think he made the substitution to differ it from the biblical recipe.

In the Jewish tradition, the olive is a symbol of domestic happiness and security, myrrh is sacred to the Lord, calamus is known for its sweetness and represents fertility and love, while cinnamon is favored for its warming ability.

In Hoodoo, these symbolisms are slightly different: myrrh and olive remain unchanged, but cinnamon is used for money and luck, and calamus is used to subtly control others. If we include Mather's galangal root in the mix, we find a root that is used for protection and court case work. In Hoodoo, galangal is widely known as 'Chewing John,' or 'Little John to Chew.' An old Hoodoo trick for winning a court case is to chew some galangal and spit the juice on the courtroom floor as you enter. Today, most practitioners suggest adding a few pieces inside your shoes before making a court appearance.

When choosing your herbs and plants, use organic whenever you can. Insecticide lingering in a bottle of anointing oil doesn't sound very magical to me. This isn't always possible so you may have to bend the rules now and then. In our shop, we try to stock herbs and teas that are organic or wild-crafted and, whenever we can, fair-trade. Always use dried herb and flowers. Fresh plant material will decay in your bottle, leaving behind a gooey bacterial mess that cannot be used.

I have listed many of the raw ingredients used in magical oils and their top purposes. This is by no means a complete list, as there are many more plants and minerals to choose from for your magical workings. However, these are the ones we stock in our retail store because they are the most requested and seem to be used more often than other rare elements. Also, be aware that the descriptions are simply the basics of what the plant is used for. You will find many other magical and spiritual applications for each one with a little research. The benefits of each plant may also differ; depending upon the magical path you follow.

AGRIMONY – Used to reverse jinxes, curses, spells, and hexes. Overcoming fear and inner blockages; dispelling negative emotions. Use as a wash or oil to increase the effectiveness of all forms of healing rituals. Used in spellwork to reveal one's true feelings.

ALFALFA – a powerful ingredient used in money drawing work. Kept in the home to ensure there is always plenty of food and money on hand. Carry alfalfa in the wallet when doing banking or meeting a loan officer.

ALKANET – The root has a history of being used as a dye. In magic, it is used for money, business matters, and gambling luck. Can also be used to counteract those people who are trying to prevent you from being successful in money matters.

ALLSPICE BERRIES – In the tradition of Hoodoo, allspice berries are carried by those who want to bring in money from gambling winnings. In witchcraft, it is used in spells of healing, determination, and energy. To protect against the evil eye.

ALTHEA – said to bring in good spirits and to increase psychic power. Also used in rituals of protection. Also known as marshmallow leaf.

ANGELICA ROOT – is widely thought to be a powerful guardian, calling upon the power of the angels. Provides strength and power to women. Used by many people for the purpose of warding off evil and used for luck in health and family. Protects children.

BARBERRY ROOT – lay barberry across the path of an enemy to undo or lessen their effect on you. Used in protection amulets for the home and for children and is also known as Holy Thorn. Used to free yourself from the power another holds over you.

BEARBERRY – Also known as Uva Ursi, the leaves ingested as a tea are believed to increase psychic abilities and divination in modern magic. Also used in incense and Native American spiritual smokes.

BLACK MUSTARD SEED – Used primarily to interfere with baneful magical work that others are conjuring against you. Is said to help create confusion in the mind of your enemy. Sprinkle where your enemies are sure to walk. Sometimes known as the 'seed of strife and discord.'

BLUE FLAG ROOT – Used in money and prosperity work, it is sometimes identified as 'snake lily.' A member of the iris family, it is often used to create money drawing incense and is burned for that purpose along with other similar herbs and roots. Do not ingest.

BONESET – used to protect your health or undo curses that others have placed on you to effect your health. Wards off evil spirits when infused and sprinkled around the house like holy water.

BUCKEYE – Carried to bring you good luck, money, and has also been used by some in divination. In the Hoodoo tradition is said to keep you in 'pocket money.' Also used as a charm for male potency. Others use in gambling and rub the Buckeye before rolling dice.

BRIMSTONE – Brimstone, (Sulphur powder) in used in magic to prevent a hex from taking hold. Destroys an enemy's power over you. Used in hex removal and spells of banishing. An ingredient in the famed 'goofer dust.'

BURDOCK – used for protection and cleansing. String

the burdock root into a necklace for protection or the larger roots can be carved into a protective amulet. Wards off negativity.

CALAMUS ROOT – In Hoodoo, calamus is used for controlling another person or a situation and is often employed in spells of domination. To bend the will of another. In the tradition of witchcraft, it is used in spells for healing and to increase the power of a spell. Do not ingest.

CALENDULA – good for dream pillows and for protection when fashioned into wreaths that are placed above doorways. Also known as 'pot marigold.' Used in home protection when blended with urine and placed at the four corners of your property. In Hoodoo, used for winning court cases.

CASCARA SAGRADA BARK – Used in legal matters and court case work. It is said that you should create an infusion from the bark and surround your property with it before going to court. Burning on a charcoal the day before a court date is said to increase your chances of winning.

CATNIP – used in spells for beauty and happiness, Catnip is also used to capture the heart of another and make them yours. Used for attraction spells.

CHAMOMILE – used to attract money and for gamblers to ensure winnings. Often used for sleep and meditation, but can also be sprinkled around your home and property to remove spells cast against you.

CHEWING JOHN – Also known as "Little John," it is the third in line of the 'John' roots after 'High John' and 'Low John.' Most often used in court case work and is actually chewed. The saliva that is produced is the element used in the spellwork.

CHICORY – used to remove all obstacles in your path that prevent you from your hopes, dreams, and aspirations. Carrying chicory on the body is said to help with gaining favors from others. Told to help with unlocking inner strength and powers. Told to make one invulnerable and bring success.

CINNAMON CHIPS – brings money to you quickly and is used in all forms of money drawing magic. When burned as an incense, it is said to raise protective vibrations. Good luck, energy, consecration, and for divination.

COLTSFOOT – used in spells of tranquility and peace. When burned as an incense, is thought to increase psychic visions and clear away foggy thoughts and mental issues.

COMFREY – often used in spells for making sure you hold onto the money you already have. Used for travel safety and is placed in suitcases to ensure your baggage is not lost. Used for car safety by creating a sachet that is hung from the rearview mirror. Wards off the evil of unknown strangers and protects from theft.

DAMIANA – known as the 'love herb' it is especially useful in lust magic. Used to increase passion and spark an old love interest. Strong herb for use in all forms of sexuality magic.

DANDELION – for promoting psychic powers and to send messages to loved ones telepathically. Often used in dream pillows for psychic dreaming and sleep protection. Often used in divination, wishing, and calling upon spirits.

DEVILS DUNG – Used to keep evil away from you and

keep you off the radar of the law. Also used as a baneful ingredient to bring harm to your enemies or to keep them from bothering you. Has been used as an incense for protection and exorcism. Also known as asafoetida.

DIXIE JOHN ROOT – Also known as "Low John" and "Southern John." Dixie John is used for matters that involve family life and love. Utilized to enhance your sex life and as a breakup ingredient against those who threaten your marriage. Also known as Beth root.

DOG GRASS ROOT – Can sometimes be found as 'couch grass,' which is usually used to draw in a new lover. Dog grass and dog grass root, however, is used primarily as a 'break up' ingredient. Most often used in moving candle spells for breakup work. A doll baby ingredient for controlling a lover.

ELECAMPANE – Mixed with mistletoe and vervain, it is said to make a powerful love powder in Santeria and Hoodoo. Related to the daisy, other words for this plant are elf wort, elf dock, and Indian pipe. Said to protect against witches when mixed with mugwort and nettle.

FENNEL – hung in doors and windows, fennel is said to protect the home from spirits and can be carried with you for the same purpose. Used for the prevention of curses and the keep the law at bay. Also used for confidence and courage.

FENUGREEK – often used in money drawing spells and mixtures. Said to bring money into the house by dropping a few fenugreek seeds into the mop water. For prosperity, obtaining salary increases, and with help in finding money.

FIVE FINGER GRASS – Known especially for good luck in money and love. Legend says to carry a little with you if you are going to ask a favor of someone. Also used to expel evil. Ingredient in money mojo bags. Brew as a tea and wash the hands and forehead nine times to remove hexes.

GINGER ROOT – used in spells of success and achievement. Said to increase the power of a spell by chewing ginger root or drinking ginger tea before performing a spell or ritual. Used for money attraction, to raise the desire in a relationship, and for general protection.

GRAINS OF PARADISE – Used for good luck, protection, making wishes and seeking gainful employment. Carry grains of paradise in your pocket during a job interview is said to bring success. Also known as Guinea Grains, many people use them exclusively for gambling.

GRAVEL ROOT – used to obtain steady work and should be carried when applying for a new job. Include as one of the main ingredients in a mojo bag in preparation for asking for a raise. Also used to remove tension from within the home.

HIBISCUS – used for love and marriage spells, hibiscus can also be drunk as a tea to promote sexual attraction and increase desire. Sometimes used for divination, to raise clairvoyant abilities, and to attract good spirits while keeping evil ones away.

HIGH JOHN THE CONQUEROR ROOT – Often used in mojo bags, High John is a must for African American folk magic. For mastery, power, drawing luck, masculine energy, sexuality, money, strength and is used in domination spells. Wash hands with an infusion of High John before games of chance and gambling.

HONEYSUCKLE FLOWERS – used to bind a love interest to you. When infused in oil, can be used to anoint the forehead to increase psychic vision. Placed around green candles with cinnamon and alfalfa to attract money.

HOPS – often used in dream magic to increase visions during sleep. Also to promote a more peaceful sleep while dreaming. Helps keep away nightmares.

HYSSOP – probably the number one unhexing herb, it is often used in spiritual baths to remove curses and hexes or to 'baptize' you as new when seeking a change. Purification and cleansing. Hung in the home to expel negativity and evil influences.

JASMINE FLOWERS – said to increase the power of love magic when included as one of the ingredients in your love spell. Helps to bring on new ideas and enhance prophetic dreams. Often used for attracting your soul mate in spells cast to find 'the right one.'

JUNIPER BERRY – mainly used as an herb of protection, it is also used to prevent theft. Utilized in rites of exorcism and can be used the same way to expel negative influences from your life. Also to attract a sexual partner.

LADY'S MANTLE – The patron herb of alchemy, Lady's Mantle enhances whatever magic you are performing. Used in love spells, potions, and amulets for attracting love. For connection to the Feminine or Goddess energy.

LAVENDER – a flower of friendship and harmony. While lavender is often included in love spells, it also helps to strengthen the bonds of friendship. Used to assist with sleep and rest and is also helpful in centering the mind for scrying. Worn to attract a new man or as protection from a cruel spouse. Also used in healing mixtures, to help see spirits, and is a powerful ingredient in purification baths. In aromatherapy, lavender is used for relaxation and to calm the body and mind. It is sometimes associated with the third-eye chakra, which is why it is used to center the mind for scrying and divination.

LEMON BALM – used to soothe emotional pain, especially after the end of a relationship. Also known as 'Melissa.' Helps calm the mind for those with nervous or mental disorders and can be used for clarity and focus. Soothes the mind for meditation and ritual.

LEMON PEEL – a tea made of lemon peel can be used as a wash to cleanse ritual tools and new items purchased. Also used to remove old conditions and give way for new things to appear. For purification, cleansing, and to magically cleanse the home. Evil eye protection.

LEMON VERBENA – Wear to attract the opposite sex. On the flip side, can be used to clear away old conditions and rid yourself of unwanted people. Often used in spells that help people break bad habits and addictions. Also used to cleanse a space and remove negative energy.

LEMONGRASS – is used in spiritually cleansing the home and is found in such products as Van Van oil and Chinese Wash. Said to help cleanse out jinxes and scrub away residual negative energy in a home or business. Can also be used to bathe amulets and ritual tools and is sometimes used in the development of psychic powers.

LICORICE ROOT – used in love and lust magic to ensure fidelity and to command the other person to bend to your will. For this reason, it is often used in spells that compel another to follow you or do your bidding. Used for taking control over situations and for spells of domination.

LODESTONE – has been used as a powerful amulet and Good Luck charm. It supposed to attract power, favors, love, money, and gifts. Can help to attract and brings into your life the things you want. Also known as a grounding stone.

LILY OF THE VALLEY – Conscious mind, memory, mental healing, peace, tranquility, purity. Can be used in rituals / spells to stop harassment. Can be used to promote longevity in marriage. Expands feelings of peace and comfort. Memory enhancing. Do not ingest.

LOVAGE ROOT – used to make one more attractive and alluring to anyone who looks upon them. To make one ache for you, mix lovage with Queen Elizabeth root and High John and bathe in for 9 days straight or take the same ingredients to make a mojo bag for love. An oil infusion of lovage is good for anointing candles of attraction. Also associated with psychic dreaming and purification.

MANDRAKE ROOT – Place mandrake root above the mantle in the home for protection and prosperity. Said to expel and repel demons. In Hoodoo, tie mandrake root to a doll baby and it is said to bind your love to you. Others wrap a dollar bill around Mandrake to bring in money. Also used for fertility, protection, and a gambling good luck charm.

MUGWORT – Burned and inhaled for psychic abilities, made into a tea to wash amulets and crystals. Place around divination and scrying tools to increase their power or near the bed to enable astral travel.

MULLEIN – sometimes ground and used in place of graveyard dirt. Often used in dark magic spells and to raise spirits. On the flip side of the coin, mullein is hung over doorways as a powerful barrier against demons and evil spirits. Protection against nightmares.

NETTLE – powerful protector. Use nettle to break a jinx and send it back to the one who cast it. Worn as a talisman to keep negativity away. Used as an ingredient in purification baths.

NUTMEG – One of the money drawing botanicals, nutmeg is most often used in games of chance. Many use the whole nutmeg inside a money mojo bag and carry with them for gambling luck. Also used as a luck charm, they are sometimes strung with star anise and worn as a necklace.

PEONY ROOT – used to draw in good fortune and protect against misfortune. Worn on the body, it protects the body and soul from evil spirits and is also used to guard the home. Strung as a necklace to be worn by children for protection. Used for prosperity and success in business. Exorcism and to remove bad spirits.

PEPPERMINT – used for healing and purification, peppermint has also been used as a rub or wash on doors and furniture to expel negativity and evil. Protects the home against illness. Spread peppermint around the altar for help in performing magic.

PLANTAIN – For healing, strength, and protection. Also known as Snakeweed because it is said to ward off snakes when carried in the pockets. Used in spells to ward off sickness and death.

PYRITE – often called 'Fools Gold' it is a mineral used in money magic. It guards against control and manipulation by a boss, lover, parent, or spouse. Prized by the Native Americans as a healing stone of magic. Used for good luck and much fortune.

QUEEN ELIZABETH ROOT – Also known as Orris root. Most often used to attract men and have them fall in love with the one who carries the root. Promotes popularity, success, and aids in communication.

RED CLOVER – Most often used in marriage and love spells, it also magically secures a good sex life. Used in baths for finance magic. Money, fidelity, success, luck. An infusion of red clover is said to help remove evil spirits.

RED PEPPER FLAKES – Most often used in enemy work, it is an ingredient used in 'Hot Foot' work, and some sprinkle it directly in the path of where their nemesis would walk. A traditional ingredient in souring jars as well. Magically, it is used to create an uncomfortable heat.

RED SANDALWOOD – Magical uses of red sandalwood include removing negativity, increasing opportunities and bringing success. Red sandalwood is a popular incense wood, often burned during spells for protection, healing & exorcism.

ROSE PETALS – used to induce dreams of one's future love. The main ingredient used in love spells. For emotions and divinity. To build a long lasting relationship.

ROSEMARY – often used in spells of fidelity and to end jealousy. Used often for ritual cleansing by steeping rosemary in the bath water. Protection, Purification. Is also used in handfastings as a symbol of love and loyalty.

RUE – In Santeria, rue is one of the main ingredients used in purification rituals. In witchcraft and Hoodoo, it is a powerful protection herb and is often used in the crafting of talisman for that purpose. Can be sprinkled around the home or your property to protect a space.

SAGE LEAF, RUBBED – This is garden sage, not white sage. Regular garden sage is for wisdom and guidance in making decisions. White sage was not always available to all regions, so regular garden sage was burned to cleanse and purify a space. Said to help with courage and strength, as well as to weaken the ego of another.

SARSAPARILLA – used in love spells and to draw in money. Often used for health and as an ingredient for house blessings. Practiced in spells to prolong life, increase passion and sexuality, and to improve virility.

SENNA – used to draw in the love of a stranger or to intensify an existing love. Enhances the flow of love when used with other love spell ingredients.

VANDAL ROOT (VALERIAN) – use to end quarrels and create a peaceful household. Sometimes used as a replacement for graveyard dirt. Also used for darker magic to summon demons and spirits and as an ingredient in baneful spells.

VERBENA – often used for drawing in new love and breaking jinxes. Used in spells to break bad habits and addictions. Used in glamour spells and for bringing inner beauty to the surface.

VIOLET LEAF – Calms the nerves, draws prophetic dreams and visions, stimulates creativity, and promotes peace and tranquility. Violet leaf provides protection from all evil. Used for love and romance work and to heal a broken heart.

WALNUT, BLACK – used in spells of astral travel. Also for baneful work such a hexing and breakup work.

WORMWOOD – also known as Absinthe. Said to increase psychic powers, evocation, divination, scrying, and prophecy. Exorcism, binding, protection. Burned with mugwort to call upon helpful spirits. Supposed to help prevent accidents. External use only.

YARROW – used for healing, courage, self-esteem, and for overcoming fear. Taking a ritual bath with yarrow is said to increase psychic abilities. Also used to break curses.

WAYS TO USE MAGICAL AND SPIRITUAL OILS

The application of spiritual oils is practiced in many ways, for many reasons — not just for anointing the head. But remember that, while the ingredients for the oils come from nature, a great many are not meant for internal use. So, no bright ideas about drinking them down like a potion in a movie. Keep them on the surface of candles, property, magical tools, and yourself. Safety comes first.

ANOINTING - here we turn to the old tried and true

method of using spiritual oils. When anointing yourself or someone else, it is believed that it is best to rub the oil in a downward motion. If you anoint the arms, rub downward towards the hands. For the head, begin at the top of the head and move towards the chest. Then, from the legs down towards the feet and so on. The entire body doesn't have to be anointed each time, as it can depend on the type of prayer or ritual you are performing. Many people still use the oil to make the sign of the cross on the forehead. A simple method is to include a few drops of oil to the bath water.

CANDLE DRESSING - I think it is important to mention the direction a candle should be dressed with oil. When you want things to come into your life, you rub the oils on the candle from bottom to top. When you desire for situations to exit your life, you rub the oils from the top of the candle towards the bottom. Upwards attracts the things you want, downward clears them out. State a focused prayer, petition, or intention while dressing your candle then light.

MARKING THE HOUSE - this type of oil application is most often used in spells of protection, cleansing or blessing. It is best to give your home a full spiritual cleansing before marking it with spiritual oils. Many people use white sage to cleanse the space while others turn to the Hoodoo practice of cleansing with what are known as 'floor washes.' The most widely known is the traditional Chinese Wash, a natural liquid soap with magical ingredients added. It is diluted with water and used to clean the house physically. I know many people who clean with Chinese wash first and sage afterward. Think of it as a spiritual Spring cleaning. Once the home is physically cleaned, the anointing can begin. A substantial amount of oil is not needed and can make a mess if you go overboard. Just touch your fingertip to the lip of the bottle and get a few drops of oil. Use the oil to mark around door frames, window frames, door knobs, and thresholds. When you have covered the entire house, mark the outside frames of your doors. If you have a porch or patio, anoint the four corners as well. I've always found it helpful to use protection oils on the welcome mat.

APPLY TO OBJECTS - the first thing that comes to mind for me is how 'Money Drawing' oil is used. I forever tell customers in our shop to rub it on wallets and purses because they are directly associated with money. You might rub a few drops of 'Passion and Lust' oil on the inside corners of your lingerie drawer or 'Boss Control' oil around your cubicle at work. A drop of 'Healing Energy' oil would be fabulous on a bottle of medicine. Whenever I buy a new Tarot deck, I rub a small amount of 'Psychic Vision' oil on my fingertips and run it along the outside edges of the deck - not enough to make the cards oily but just enough for it to be present. You can also use specific oils to anoint your magical tools. New statuary, ritual knives, stones and crystals, wands — anything you will be using in your workings. During Mercury-in-Retrograde, place some Van-Van oil (said to turn bad luck into good) on the tires of your car or around your computer to protect them from breaking down.

ON PETITION PAPERS – a petition is a written statement of intention or a prayer. It states clearly your wish or what you expect to happen. It might include someone's name, symbols, sigils, your purpose, or all of these. When they only include names, they are sometimes referred to as simply 'name papers.' They are used under candles, inside mojo bags, and inside jar and bottle spells. Some people will place their petition inside a locket. Petitions can also be written over the photographs of people involved in your spell or prayer work. One

Hoodoo tradition is to tear off a piece of a brown paper bag to use for a petition paper. It is customary to make sure the paper is hand-torn on all sides and that no machine-cut edges be left intact. Spiritual oils can be used on petition papers to imbue them with the powers the herbs and other ingredients contain. Often blotted in the sign of the cross or at the four corners of the paper.

NOTE about using pictures and photographs in spellwork: You may use photocopied pictures or images printed from your computer. Since many spells require that you write on, fold up, or sometimes tear the picture, there is no need to destroy a perfectly good photograph that you cannot replace. It is the imagery of the person(s) that matters – not that it be an original photo.

FEEDING MOJO BAGS - First, you might ask, what is a mojo bag? In simple terms, it is a prayer or spell in a bag. Creating one, however, is more complex. Inside there may be a variety of ingredients: herbs, minerals, bones, flowers, and sometimes personal items like a locket of hair. When made for a specific purpose or person, a mojo bag usually contains a petition (a written prayer or intention). In the Hoodoo tradition, we customarily use the term 'mojo bag, ' but it can be called by many other names: a mojo hand, gris-gris bag, toby, or trick bag. Usually made of red flannel, some practitioners prefer to choose a color that relates to its use. For example, a money mojo might be green. But tradition dictates that it is almost always made of flannel. Another belief is that it is best to include an odd number of ingredients such as 3, 5, 7, 13, etc. Some people use an actual drawstring bag to create their mojo. My preferred method is what is known as a 'flaming comet' style mojo bag where a square of flannel is gathered up around the ingredients and tied off with string or twine. It should be made small enough to carry on your person. After it is created, it is fed with a liquid of some sort. While many use Florida water cologne or some other type of alcohol, I am one of those who prefers to feed the bag with condition oil — one that corresponds to the nature of the mojo bag. A love mojo, for example, should be fed with love oil. The bag is carried with you to impart its magic into your life. For the first three days, it should be kept against your skin and placed under your pillow at night. Keep your mojo a secret and never let another touch it. And, by all means, never open your mojo bag once it is made. Magically speaking, this is the act of killing your mojo bag. As the weeks go on and if your petition doesn't seem to be manifesting, it may be time to feed your mojo bag again. Simply rub a little oil on the bag whenever you feel it needs a magical lift.

SECRETIVE USES - there are also many ways to apply magical oils in secret for an intended purpose. To strengthen the marital bond, one might offer their spouse a neck rub and include a few drops of 'Adam and Eve' oil to lotion or massage oil. To spice things up a bit, rub a little 'Passion and Lust' oil on your partner's favorite bar of soap so that they will rub it all over their naked body. Have a loud or nosy neighbor? Brush a small amount of 'Hot Foot' oil on the very edges of a Christmas card and allow it to dry. When completely dry, mail it to the neighbor. If the slight cinnamon smell lingers on the card, don't worry about it — after all, cinnamon is a scent used during the Christmas season. It is an old Hoodoo trick for a woman to dab a little of her vaginal fluid behind each ear and top it off with 'Come to Me' oil whenever she is near the man she wants to attract.

Before we proceed with ways to use your oils in spells, rituals, and everyday life, I want to go over the list of oils most often used. Since I will be referencing them in many of the magical workings, it seems best to familiarize yourself with them ahead of time. There are several excellent creators of oils out there, and, quite frankly, some inferior ones. It is unfortunate that there are individuals and companies who create spiritual oils only for their novelty and for the profit. Unless it is mixed by a knowledgeable practitioner who truly puts their intention and energy into the oils creation, and with the proper training about which ingredients should be used magically — I'm afraid that all you will end up with is just a scented bottle of oil.

I cannot speak to oils I have never tried and won't attempt to. That trial and error must be in your hands. My husband and I both create our own line of spiritual oils. His line is sold under his **Spirit Essentials** label, while my own is found under my **White Mojo** brand name. Both of us are not only magical practitioners but also certified aromatherapists. I also took a course in perfumery some years ago. Our main company, the **aromagregory soap & tea company (aromaG's Botanica** for short) has been around since 1999. So, as you can see, we know our way around herbs and oils. **The Lucky Mojo Curio Company** in Forestville, California is another trusted source. The proprietor, Catherine Yronwode, is a walking encyclopedia on the topic of Hoodoo. Part of my training in this magical art came from her.

First, we will cover the White Mojo line of oils. I created them in the Hoodoo tradition of magic. Many of their names are reminiscent of the old Hoodoo oils and formulas found in catalogs of the 1920's and 1930's. I do want to go over the way I formulate my oils because it is a fascinating process. First, I decide what type of oil I will be compounding and write down all of the ingredients used for that particular situation, problem, or condition. When my list is complete, I take a pencil and close my eyes, asking Spirit to guide me through crossing items off the list. When I open my eyes again, the ingredients left unmarked become the formula for the oil. I then decide which ingredients will be used in the form of essential oils, and which ones will be dried herbs. After placing the dried elements in the bottle, I add the essential oils one drop at a time, allowing my intuition to guide me, writing down each one before moving to the next. Since the oils are propriety blends, I never reveal all of their ingredients, which is why you will often find the words 'and other herbs and essential oils...' All of our magical oil blends are in a base of fractioned coconut oil, as shown in their descriptions.

HOODOO OILS

ADAM AND EVE

This oil is most often used in Hoodoo to strengthen a marriage or to heal one. Some use it in conjunction with Reconcile products to bring a marriage back together. Can also be used to strengthen a partnership. It is an excellent oil for when a marriage or partnership is showing signs of decay and the people involved need to find their connection to each other again, their bond. While it is sometimes used for people who are apart or have broken up, it is more successful when the couple is still physically together. Sometimes used to seal the bonds of a business relationship. Hibiscus flowers, lavender, patchouli, orange, lemongrass, and other herbs and essential oils in a base of fractionated coconut oil.

Candle color = pink

ATTRACT

Attraction oil is meant for attracting all things to you whether it be love, money, luck, success, or whatever you desire. It is a flexible Hoodoo blend to bring good things your way. A major plus of Attract oil is its flexibility in regards to being mixed with other oils. For example, mix it with Money Drawing oil for attracting money making opportunities. With lodestone, pyrite, peony root, five finger grass, cardamom, calamus, orange oil, and other herbs and essential oils in a base of fractioned coconut oil.

Candle color = orange

BANISH NEGATIVITY

The Banish Negativity Oil is meant to help dampen the effects of negative people around you. Place at the four corners of your front door and add a little to the doormat to keep negative people away from your home or anoint yourself to keep these people at bay. I always suggest using this oil when you have a lot of nay-sayers in your life, people who drag you down with their negative talk. Keep it on you whenever you must be around these characters. Bay leaf, burdock, hyssop, lemon oil, and other herbs and essential oils in a base of fractioned coconut oil.

Candle color = black

BLESSING

This oil can be used in a variety of ways: as a primary anointing oil to bring forth blessings, to help create advantages and positive energy to enter another's life, or to bless an object that you hold sacred. Used in magic when you want to install goodness into a situation. Can also be used in prayer. For anointing ritual or holy tools and to purify altars. Angelica root, passion flower, frankincense, sweet marjoram, lemongrass, and other herbs and essential oils in a base of fractionated coconut oil.

Candle color = white

BOSS CONTROL

Boss Control is used to make your employer see things your way and side in your favor. Rub on the doorway of your office, cubicle, or desk. Whenever we hire a new employee in the store, I always joke with them that they are forbidden to buy the Boss Control oil. Anoint yourself before important meetings. Angelica root, five finger grass, alfalfa, chamomile, thyme, cedarwood, and other herbs and essential oils in a base of fractionated coconut oil.

Candle color = orange

BREAK UP

Not just for breaking up a couple of lovers but also for ending bad business relationships quickly. Most people turn to break up work when they want two lovers to separate. But, when using it to make two business associates part ways, it is usually best to carefully plan ahead what type of spell or ritual you will use the oil with. After all, a business should be dissolved fairly. Meaning, the company shouldn't break up because one partner emptied the bank accounts and left the country, leaving the other high and dry. When it is used in a romantic sense (because you want one of the parties to leave and come to you), people overlook that they should simultaneously be performing Love Attracting or Come to Me work. Just because two people break up, it doesn't mean the one you desire will come running in your direction. Jezebel root, Dixie John root, red pepper, litsea oil, eucalyptus, cedarwood, and other herbs and essential oils in a base of fractionated coconut oil.

Candle color = black

BUST IT DOWN

This oil is sometimes also known as Blockbuster oil. It is most often used for breaking down obstacles in your way, no matter what they are. Magically used for removing emotional and physical roadblocks that hold back your success. Many of life's roadblocks appear in the form of emotional blockages: low self-esteem, procrastination, grief, and perfectionism are a few examples. Perhaps an addiction is holding you back. Maybe it is the people around you that feel safer by keeping you within their little box. Removing your obstacles is the first step to success. Perform separate magical work to achieve the goal you desire, once the restriction is removed. Lemongrass, five finger grass, lemon oil, litsea oil, marjoram oil, basil oil, and other herbs and essential oils in a base of fractionated coconut oil.

Color candle = orange

CAST OUT AND BANISH

Cast Out and Banish oil is for when you want to get a particular person OR situation out of your life as well as evil outside influences. When you want someone or something to leave your home or space, you cast them out, banish them. Not just for people and circumstances. When I formulated this oil, it was designed to be used in the physical and the astral sense. So, in conjunction with other well-known methods (such as burning white sage), it is often used for removing unwanted spirits from the home. Angelica, white sage, frankincense, clove, birch, nettle, peony, and other herbs and essential oils in a base of fractioned coconut oil.

Candle color = gray

CLEARING & UNBLOCKING

Clearing and Unblocking oil is meant to clear out and unblock old messages from the past – things that hold you back. Clears those negative voices that say to you, "I can't do it." Good oil for wiping a slate clean. For example, someone in your past told you that you had no artistic talent, which caused you to stop creating art. This is a voice from the past. The only way to reach our full potential is to leave behind the boundaries other people set for us. Could also be used to tackle phobias. White sage, cloves, myrrh, lavender buds, ylang-ylang oil, coriander seeds, and other herbs and essential oils in a base of fractioned coconut oil.

Candle color = white

COME TO ME

WHITE MOJO
NASHVILLE TENNESSEE

COME TO ME

Come to Me oil is a formula blended for exactly what it sounds like: to bring another person to you. To attract a new lover or to draw in a specific person into your life. Most of the time, this oil is worn whenever you plan to be around a particular person and want them to notice you. When that person is at a distance, it is used on candles and prayer papers (petitions) to make them think about you and desire to be with you. There are occasions, however, when the oil is used to draw someone back into your life that is not a love interest such as old friends and people from the past you no longer have a connection with. Lodestone, catnip, damiana, geranium, Queen Elizabeth root, patchouli, lemon, and other herbs and essential oils in a base of fractioned coconut oil.

Candle color = pink

COMMAND

to help bring another under your control or bring them around to your way of thinking. Some sell this oil as Commanding oil. Its energy says, "you will do as I tell you to do." To influence others. Chewing John, peony root, licorice root, frankincense oil, bay oil, bergamot oil, and other herbs and essential oils in a base of fractionated coconut oil.

Candle color = dark blue

CONFIDENCE BOOSTING

Whether you are speaking in public or just need more confidence in everyday matters, Confidence Boosting oil is meant to keep you calm, collected, and confident. Know what you want, say it out loud, and go out in the world and get it. A good oil for tackling matters of self-esteem or to help overcome shyness. Ginger root, peony root, black pepper, sweet marjoram oil, mandarin oil, and other herbs and essential oils in a base of fractioned coconut oil.

Candle color = blue

CONFUSION

When people see this oil, they mistakenly think it is for alleviating confusion. On the contrary, this oil is to create confusion and scatter the thoughts of those who are working against you to weaken their baneful efforts. So, in simple terms, it is an oil of influence, meant to break the concentration of your nemesis. Red pepper, broom straws, sage, lemongrass, valerian, eucalyptus, and other herbs and essential oils in a base of fractioned coconut oil.

Candle color = brown

COURAGE & BRAVERY

Slightly different than Confidence Boosting oil, this blend was created to give you the courage to go after everything you want in life and the bravery to follow through with all your efforts to achieve those goals. It is a goal-oriented recipe. John the Conqueror root, myrrh, peony, wintergreen, calamus, bergamot, and other herbs and essential oils in a base of fractioned coconut oil.

Candle color = blue

COURT CASE

These ingredients are said to help you with a judge or jury. Use on your body the day of court. Used before a court date to work magic on the opposing attorney, the judge, or both. If you were working on both, do it with separate spells. For the opposing attorney, do magic to undermine his efforts. On the judge, you will work more towards having him favor you. Tobacco, oregano, tansy, bergamot, Chewing John, bay rum, dill, and other herbs and essential oils in a base of fractioned coconut oil.

Candle color = brown

CROSSING

Crossing oils have been used in Hoodoo for working against your enemies or those who mean you harm. Used for laying tricks and bringing on crossed conditions, it is considered one of the baneful oils. In Hoodoo, there is a term known as a "Lady Hearted" rootworker - someone who won't perform baneful work against others. Based on your beliefs, only you can decide if you wish to take on this type of work. Cleansing work is usually performed on yourself after doing "negative work." Vandal root, cayenne pepper, licorice root, cedarwood oil, calamus oil, lemon oil, and other herbs and essential oils in a base of fractionated coconut oil.

Candle color = black

CROWN OF ACHIEVEMENT

Also known as Crown of Success, Crown of Achievement is used for success in career, business, and the performing arts. Especially suitable for singers, songwriters, and other performers trying to break into the business or anyone who makes their living by working with their hands. Can be used for any goal-oriented spellwork. John the Conqueror root, pyrite, frankincense, bay leaf, five finger grass, and other herbs and essential oils in a base of fractioned coconut oil.

Candle color = purple

CUT AND CLEAR

Used to break the ties of the past and cut away all remaining links to previous lovers, partners, or others that need to clear out of your life. While it sounds like magical work to affect others, its benefits are exceptional to the one performing the spell. Clearing out your mind of old grudges, resentments, and ties to things that no longer matter are a necessity to moving forward. This is why we want to cut out all of the old baggage and open the path to a new and bright future. Lemon balm, black pepper, hyssop, lemongrass, rosemary, eucalyptus, palmarosa, and other herbs and essential oils in a base of fractioned coconut oil.

Candle color = gray

DARK ARTS

oil is used in spell work of a baneful nature to aid in destructive and somewhat negative rituals. Some refer to it as Black Arts. Used in cursing or hexing work, sometimes alongside hot foot work, or any other ceremony that works magic against an enemy or those who mean you harm. Frankincense, mugwort, peppermint, frankincense oil, cedarwood oil, and other herbs and essential oils in a base of fractionated coconut oil.

Candle color = black

DEVIL BE GONE

this Hoodoo oil is used in prayer and spell work and is said to keep the devil and his helpers at bay. It is to keep harmful elements out of your life to make room for the good. Some use it against inner demons such as jealousy, gluttony, resentment, addiction, etc. Angelica, blessed thistle, allspice, lemongrass, rosemary oil, black pepper oil, lemongrass oil, and other herbs and essential oils in a base of fractionated coconut oil.

Candle color = white or red

DOMINATE

used in Hoodoo and magical rituals dealing with dominating and ruling others. Is said to aid in controlling others to do your will. Often used with COMMAND oil to double its effects. Dominate oil uses some of the same energy as Command but takes it a step further, demanding that the person you are working on take your thoughts, feelings, and opinions into consideration before making any of their own decisions. Licorice root, angelica root, frankincense, cedarwood oil, calamus oil, bergamot, and other herbs and essential oils in a base of fractionated coconut oil.

Candle color = orange

FOLLOW ME GAL

is said to make women follow a man around and desire him. Has been sold since the 1920's and 1930's, mainly in novelty catalogs that catered to believers and followers of Hoodoo. Use as a personal scent on the body or as an anointing oil for candles. This is the oil used by MEN to get the attention of women. (for the opposite effect, see our Follow Me Guy — worn by women.) To peak a woman's interest to the point where she wants to be around you all the time. Catnip, juniper berry, sandalwood oil, vanilla absolute, orange oil, and other herbs and essential oils in a base of fractionated coconut oil.

Candle color = red or pink

FOLLOW ME GUY

to make men follow a woman around and desire her. Use as a personal scent on the body or as an anointing oil for candles. This is the oil used by WOMEN to get the attention of men. (for the opposite effect, see our Follow Me Gal — worn by men.) The concept is that the man who is your target will follow you around like a puppy dog, wanting nothing more than to please you. Catnip, orris root, rose petals, ylang-ylang oil, patchouli oil, lavender oil, orange oil and other herbs and essential oils in a base of fractionated coconut oil.

Candle color = red or pink

GOOD LUCK

Good Luck oil is used for general good luck and also in gambling. Luck oils have been around for quite a while. Often used before a job interview or before buying lottery tickets. A good oil to use during those times when you feel nothing seems to be going your way, and your luck needs to turn around. This good luck oil contains High John Conqueror root, holly, rosehips, star anise, cypress oil, and other herbs and essential oils blended in a base of fractionated coconut oil.

Candle color = blue

HAPPY HOME

Used to create a loving, warm, and friendly home environment. The safety of the home creates a mood for all those under its roof. Used to help make others calm, helpful, and loving towards each other. Good for family life. Anoint the four corners of the house, both inside and outside. Burn on white or yellow candles around the house from time to time to keep the good energy flowing. Anoint the corners of your welcome mat. Lavender, rosemary, basil, sweet marjoram, and other herbs and essential oils in a blend of fractionated coconut oil.

Candle color = white or yellow

HEALING ENERGY

Healing energy oil is an excellent blend for people who perform energy work such as Reiki and Healing Touch therapy. Also for everyone when it comes to a little self-healing – not only physical but when you are feeling mentally drained and in need of spiritual repair. Used on the effigy of an ill person with the intention of healing. The "voodoo doll" was originally used for healing purposes - not for cursing. Oils and herbs were used on or sew into the body of the figure in the location of an ailment. Myrrh, lemon, plantain, niaouli, spearmint, and other herbs and essential oils in a base of fractioned coconut oil.

Candle color = blue

HOT FOOT

Hot Foot is used when you want to get rid of someone. Whether it be the ex that just won't leave you alone, a tenant that refuses to pay the rent, or people in your life that are always stirring up drama. When you want someone to hit the road, you "hotfoot" them. Hot Foot powder is mainly used in foot track magic and is sprinkled in the path of the person you are targeting. When they walk through it, the magical elements stick to the bottom of their shoes, "hot footing" them. Cayenne pepper, black pepper, thyme, red chilis, and other herbs and essential oils in a base of fractioned coconut oil.

Candle color = red or black

HOUSE BLESSING

House blessing oil is used when you move into a new house or apartment. However, can also be used when you are feeling like the energy in your home is not "flowing" and something needs a little pick-me-up. Useful when a negative person has been in your home. Often used after a house has been smudged with white sage to mark around the windows, door frames, and thresholds. Pine needles, white sage, passion flower, lavender and chamomile, and other herbs and essential oils in a base of fractioned coconut oil.

Candle color = yellow

JINX BEGONE

Can also be called an unhexing oil. Used to remove crossed conditions to set things on the right path again. Often used to turn around a run of bad luck. Jinx Begone is different than UNCROSS AND REVERSE because it isn't intended to send the hex back to the sender. Instead, it focuses all of its energy towards shedding the jinx from a person, place, or family. Contains hyssop, angelica, litsea, dill, patchouli, spearmint, and other herbs and essential oils in a base of fractionated coconut oil. Candle color = black or white

KISS ME QUICK

is meant to rekindle marital fires or to bring about a quick love affair. Can be used to anoint candles along with the picture of your intended or can be worn on the pulse points as a perfume and wear around your loved one. To get the sexual attention of another. Lodestone, damiana, rose petals, lavender, patchouli, and other herbs and essential oils in a base of fractioned coconut oil.

Candle color = red

LAVENDER FLAME

This oil takes on the properties of love attracting, come to me, and passion and lust - except for gay couples. Comes in two different blends for both male and female. Most often used for attracting gay love and companionship. Can also be used to surround yourself with loving friends and for attracting new same gender love interests into your life. Both blends are similar with just a few minor ingredient changes. The components they share are lavender, sandalwood, patchouli, and ylang-ylang and other herbs and essential oils in a base of fractioned coconut oil.

Candle color = lavender or purple

LOVE ATTRACTING

Who doesn't need a little more love in their life? Not just for romantic love. Can also be used to surround yourself with loving friends and for attracting new people into your life. Wear it as a pulse point perfume to attract a new interest. Unlike Come To Me oil, this can be used to ask the universe to send the right person to you — not necessarily someone you already know. Your intention sets the mood for this oil whether it be used for an old love, to bring a crush closer, or for general love attracting. This love attracting oil contains: white sage, lavender buds, rose petals, rose oil, sandalwood oil, and other herbs and essential oils in a base of fractioned coconut oil.

Candle color = red or pink

MOJO No9

Used as an all-purpose oil for all types of magic and spells or to enhance the magic of other oils and ingredients. It contains a well-balanced blend of herbs and oils that approach a variety of conditions and situations in the Hoodoo tradition. Use it when you're not sure what oil you need the most or have several circumstances to tackle. Due to its flexibility, can be utilized when you have run out of another ingredient. Alone, use in spells focused on having a well-balanced life. Angelica, hyssop, lavender, frankincense, blessed thistle, mandarin oil, vanilla absolute, bay oil, patchouli oil, and other herbs and essential oils in a base of fractionated coconut oil. Candle color is also flexible, depending on your intention. red, orange, yellow, blue, black, green, purple, white.

MONEY DRAWING

For bringing more money and abundance into your home or business. Use on purses, wallets, and wherever you deal with finances and money. Money drawing work is the most requested form of rootwork, second to love. For endeavors that bring money from hard work or a service you provide. Different energetically than oils people use for gambling luck. Money drawing is usually connected to an effort that brings a monetary payoff. Fenugreek, cinnamon, alfalfa, vetiver, and other herbs and essential oils in a base of fractioned coconut oil.

Candle color = green

MONEY LASTS

is used to hold onto the money you already have while continuing to draw in more. Used to anoint green candles for bringing in prosperity and holding onto it. To protect bank accounts, investments, and income. Used to help you reach the point where you can begin saving. Some ingredients include cinnamon chips, alfalfa, chamomile flowers, patchouli, geranium and other herbs and essential oils in a base of fractioned coconut oil.

Candle color = dark green or light green

OPEN THE GATES

Rid yourself from past mistakes and make a fresh start. Busts open the gates to a new life or new project. Similar to what is called "road opener." While it sounds similar to Cut and Clear, the mood behind this oil is of a different nature. Many people use this after Cut and Clear work has finished, paving the way for new and exciting things to manifest. Used in spell work for creating opportunities. Angelica root, Chewing John, tobacco, frankincense, clary sage, wintergreen, cardamom, and other herbs and essential oils in a base of fractioned coconut oil.

Candle color = blue or white

PASSION & LUST

This one is for spicing up your love life with primal lust and heart-pounding passion. Anoint a red candle with oil for sexuality, passion, and lust. The scent of real vanilla alone is something that attracts men. Used for when your partner is a little sluggish in the lust department or to spark a new interest in the passion that once was a part of your relationship. This passion and lust blend contains angelica, rose petals, coffee bean, ylang-ylang essential oil, vanilla and other herbs and essential oils in a base of fractioned coconut oil.

Candle color = red

PROTECT ME

Used for general protection and for keeping away harm. Use around doorways and windows, in vehicles – anywhere you feel you need a little extra protection. Protection oils are used on the body, on amulets and medallions, on vehicles, and around the home. Blessed thistle, myrrh, broom straws, cloves, st. johns wort, geranium, and other herbs and essential oils in a base of fractioned coconut oil. Candle color = purple or white

PSYCHIC VISION

This oil blend is meant to awaken and amplify the third eye and increase psychic vision. Often used by Tarot readers and other psychic workers right before a session. Can help to increase vivid dreams. Use to anoint the edges of new Tarot cards, runes, pendulums, and other forms of divination used for psychic connection. Anoint the forehead before meditation or divination. Mugwort, calendula, wormwood, frankincense, bitter almond, and other herbs and essential oils in a base of fractioned coconut oil.

Candle color = lavender

RECONCILE

Reconcile Oil is sometimes known as 'Reconciliation' and is used to repair the hurt feelings that keep friends and lovers apart. Most of the time the oil is used in conjunction with a candle ritual or mojo bag. Spells of love reconciliation are probably the most asked for variety of magical work. With lodestone, violet leaves, hibiscus, lavender oil, vanilla absolute, patchouli oil, sage oil, and other herbs and essential oils in a base of fractioned coconut oil.

Candle color = pink or white

RETURN TO ME

Return to me oil has been used in Hoodoo for prayers, spells, and rituals, aimed towards bringing back a love -- especially one that has walked out of your life. Can be blended with COME TO ME oil for an extra boost or

HEALING oil to help heal the past so that a reunion is more likely to happen. Not only for the return of relationships, but it can also be used to help with lost items. Also used with love attracting and reconcile oils. Catnip, hibiscus flowers, lavender oil, litsea oil, vanilla absolute, and other herbs and essential oils in a base of fractionated coconut oil. Candle color = orange

REVENGE

Getting revenge is about punishing someone who has wronged you until you feel avenged. Its energy is one of infliction, insult, and retaliation. Used in spells to make another feel as much emotional pain as they have caused you. Sometimes used with HOT FOOT to inflict vengeance before causing another to leave your life for good. Contains chicory, mustard seed, vandal root, cedarwood, lemon, ginger, and other herbs and essential oils in a base of fractionated coconut oil.

Candle color = black

REVERSING

Reversing Hoodoo oil is to send any bad juju that has been thrown your way back to its source. Used to reverse the effects of crossing or cursing. Many people use reversing products when creating spells with mirror boxes. Turn things back from which they came. This energy is all about sending back the bad vibes someone put on you to teach them a valuable lesson. One of the best oils for use on reversing candles. Agrimony, lemongrass, rubbed sage, elder berries, eucalyptus oil, vetiver oil, lemon oil, and other herbs and essential oils in a base of fractionated coconut oil.

Candle color = black or gray

SPIRIT GUIDE

Connecting with your Spirit Guide(s) can open up new doors for you. When you actively communicate with your Guides and seek their assistance, there is usually little hesitation with the decisions you must make. A fine oil for anointing pendulums and other types of divination that you use for connecting with guides. Good for anointing quartz crystals that you keep beside the bed for receiving information through dreams. White sage, wormwood, camphor, anise, myrrh, tea tree, and other herbs and essential oils in a base of fractioned coconut oil.

Candle color = lavender or pale blue

TONGUE TIED

Tongue Tied Hoodoo oil is meant to stop others from gossiping and talking about you. Used to dress papers, anoint candles, and mojo bags to stop gossip. If you are near the people who are doing the gossiping, rub a little of the oil on an object they will touch such as door knobs, salt shaker, keys, etc. One trick is to print out the pictures of the people who are gossiping about you, anoint their pictures with the Tongue Tied oil, and place photos in a bowl of sugar to "sweeten" the people involved. Cloves, oregano, angelica root, black pepper, mandarin essential oil, geranium essential oil, and other herbs and essential oils in a base of fractioned coconut oil.

Candle color = brown

TRIPLE JOHN

Triple John incorporates the powers of the three 'John' oils used in the Hoodoo tradition and has multiple magical uses including power, luck, love-drawing, legal protection, and control. It contains High John the Conqueror root, Dixie John (Low John), and Chewing John, and other essential oils in a base of fractioned coconut oil. Used to magnify your magic and luck. So if you need to give a spell a "boost", add some Triple John.

Candle color = orange

UNCROSS & REVERSE

When magic has been used against you, this oil is used in work to uncross you – undoing your enemy's work and sending it back to them. The energy behind this oil is to not only uncross but to make your tormentor feel the same pain and trouble they caused you. This uncross and reverse blends contains hyssop, angelica, verbena, peppermint, calendula, and other herbs and essential oils in a base of fractioned coconut oil.

Candle color = black

UNLEASH CREATIVITY

The Unleash Creativity oil is literally for breaking open that creative side of you that lurks beneath the surface. Good for painters, poets, sketch artists, graphic artists, sculptors, writers – even chefs. Also used for writer's block. Tansy, violet leaves, tangerine, clary sage, clove, rosemary, and other herbs and essential oils in a base of fractioned coconut oil.

Candle color = yellow

VAN VAN OIL

is used to set wrongs right again. It turns bad luck back into good (or at least normalizes the condition) and is particularly helpful whenever that nasty Mercury in Retrograde rolls around. Van Van oil is also used to cleanse new magical and spiritual items. Lemongrass, citronella, palmarosa, vetiver, and other herbs and essential oils in a base of fractioned coconut oil.

Candle color = orange

WALL OF FIRE

used to protect against malicious spells and other forms of psychic attack. Used as a shield against your enemies. Especially helpful when you know for certain that others are working against you and you need to create a solid barrier of protection. Dragons blood resin, ginger root, angelica, red pepper, agrimony, bay leaf. Marjoram, and other herbs and essential oils in a base of fractioned coconut oil.

Candle color = red

WIN BIG

Hoodoo has a long history of people who use oils and mojo bags for luck in gambling, the lottery, and bingo. This oil contains many of the traditional ingredients found in these oils. Rub on the hands before participating in games of chance. Alfalfa, chamomile, ginger, High John the Conqueror root, gravel root, clove oil, cinnamon oil, ginger oil, and other herbs and essential oils in a base of fractionated coconut oil.

Candle color = green

JESUS THE KING

Using many of the Biblical oils, Jesus the King oil is used mainly in prayer, focus, meditation, and reflection. Can also be used to anoint rosaries and other religious items and statuary. Contains frankincense, myrrh, sandalwood, galbanum, and other herbs and essential oils in a base of fractionated coconut oil.

Candle color = white or blue

MOTHER MARY

Mother Mary anointing oil is used for all types of prayers, blessings, meditations, and novenas to the Blessed Mother. Used to anoint the body or religious items such as rosaries, statues, altars, etc. Contains frankincense, lavender, cedarwood, rose, and other herbs and essential oils in a base of fractionated coconut oil.

Candle color = white, blue, or lavender

SAINT AND ANGEL OILS

The Saint and Angel oils are formulated by Dr. Bastian - a rootworker, Certified Aromatherapist, Reiki Master, and Shamanic Practitioner under his brand name **Spirit Essentials.** Each oil was created with a great deal of research and many hours of working with Spirit to create the perfect blend of herbs and oils that resonate not only with each Saint or Angel but also with each life situation. Herbs are added to each bottle, essential oils are counted drop by drop into each bottle, and then filled with a base of fractionated coconut oil. After the bottles are filled, they are placed on Dr. Bastian's altar where they are infused with Reiki energy, and offered a Shaman blessing asking Spirit to bless them for their intended purpose and owner.

While his Spirit Essential oils can be used in the same way as the Hoodoo oils, according to each life condition, they can also be used for prayer, meditation, inner reflection, and spiritual growth. It is left up to the user of the oils to decide if they are to be applied as devotional oils or used in spellwork, or both.

CONQUEROR - St. Expedite

Conqueror oil is used to conquer your problems or your enemies. Call on St. Expedite when you need a warrior on your side. Use in combination with other workings for quick results. St. Expedite is said to have been a Roman centurion who was martyred in Turkey for being a Christian. He is considered the patron saint of speedy cases, and his feast day is April 19. You can also call on Saint Expedite for help overcome problems with procrastination. Blend contains fennel, High John, yarrow, and other herbs and essential oils in a base of fractionated coconut oil.

Petition St. Expedite to conquer your problems and fears, for quick resolutions, and to settle disagreements.

Candle color = yellow
Psalm = 37

DOMINATION - St. Martha

Domination oil is used to gain control over a person or situation. Use this oil to make others bend to your will, or cause a situation to work out in your favor. Martha was the sister of Lazarus, whom Jesus resurrected. In Latin cultures, she is associated with domination and control. In European traditions, her associations deal more with hearth and home, the preparation of food, and hospitality. Call on Saint Martha when you need to take control of a person or situation, and have the final results fall in your favor. You can also call on Saint Martha to bless family gatherings. Blend contains bergamot, tobacco, red pepper, and other herbs and essential oils in a base of fractionated coconut oil.

Petition St. Martha to conquer your enemies, for assistance during times of domestic and financial problems, and to keep a partner faithful.

Candle color = orange
Psalm = 114

GOOD LUCK - St. John the Baptist

Good Luck oil is used to bring good luck into your life, and favorable outcomes to your activities. Use this oil for gambling, job interviews, loans, searching for lost items, and general good fortune. John the Baptist was an itinerant Jewish preacher in the early first century AD. Most scholars agreed that he baptized Jesus. Some report he was the cousin of Jesus of Nazareth. In some Native American traditions, St. John the Baptist is said to be the one who draws radical attention to himself so that you might look at your own life and activities. Blend contains cardamom, five finger grass, High John, and other herbs and essential oils in a base of fractionated coconut oil.

Petition St. John the Baptist for good luck, to protect you from your enemies, and for blessings of your gardens.

Candle color = green
Psalm = 65

HAPPINESS - St. Lawrence

Happiness oil is used to promote a feeling of joy and bliss in your life. It is designed to help activate the sacral chakra, which brings us joy. Use this oil to bring gratitude into your life, and accept the blessing of the Universe. St. Lawrence was in charge of the treasures and material goods of the church, and when he distributed these treasures to the poor, he was put to death by roasting over coals. After the martyr had suffered pain for a long time, the legend concludes, he declared: "I'm well done. Turn me over!" For this, he is recognized as the patron saint of cooks, chefs, and comedians. Blend contains bergamot, pink grapefruit, marjoram, and other herbs and essential oils in a base of fractionated coconut oil.

Petition St. Lawrence for a happy home and life, and to deepen your faith.

Candle color = yellow
Psalm = 98

HEALING - St. Lazarus

Healing oil is used to promote complete healing of body, mind, emotions and spirit. It can also be used to request healing for an illness for yourself and others. Use this oil to anoint the sick and terminally ill. The story of Lazarus is one of the miracles of Jesus mentioned in the Gospel of John, in which Jesus resurrects him from death. Blend contains cypress, coltsfoot, self heal, and other herbs and essential oils in a base of fractionated coconut oil.

Petition St. Lazarus to heal the sick and preserve good health.

Candle color = blue
Psalm = 30

HOPE & FAITH - St. Jude

St. Jude is known as the Patron Saint of Desperate Cases because his letter in the New Testament taught early Christians to persevere during times of harsh and difficult circumstances. He is often called upon to heal the terminally ill. He brings us hope in times of our darkest hours. Blend contains eucalyptus, spearmint, violet and other herbs and essential oils in a base of fractionated coconut oil.

Petition St. Jude during times of hopelessness, to assist with impossible cases, to help get someone off drugs or alcohol, and to help get someone out of jail.

Candle color = white or yellow

HOUSE BLESSING - St. Joseph

House Blessing oil is used to bless and remove negativity from your home and property. It helps promote a feeling of security and removes negative entities and unwanted guests. Combined with a St. Joseph statue, this oil can assist you when trying to sell your house. St. Joseph is known in the four Gospels as the husband of Mary and the earthly father of Jesus. He provided a stable and secure earthly home for the Jewish maiden chosen by God to have his son. St. Joseph is the patron saint of workers. Joseph is regarded as a model for fathers and fatherhood. Blend contains cedarwood, white sage, rosemary, and other herbs and essential oils in a base of fractionated coconut oil.

Petition St. Joseph to sell a home, for happiness in a marriage, for protection of your home, for assistance in find employment, and for inspiration during times of doubt.

Candle color = yellow
Psalm = 108

LOVE ATTRACTING - Archangel Anael

Love Attracting oil is used to bring love into your life. Use this oil to attract that special person to you, or for general use to find your soulmate or passion partner. Archangel Anael has dominion over the air, thereby influencing love, romance, and passion. Also known as Haniel or Aniel, Archangel Anael is included in the list of archangels according to Jewish teachings, and is associated with the planet Venus, which is also connected with sexuality. Blend contains patchouli, ginger, rose petals, and other herbs and essential oils in a base of fractionated coconut oil.

Candle color = red
Psalm = 111

MEDITATION - Buddha

Meditation oil is used to aid in meditation. This oil calms the mind, focuses your thoughts, and grounds the emotions. The philosophy of Buddhism started with the teachings of Siddhartha Gautama, referred to as the Buddha. The word 'Buddha' is a title, which means 'one who is awake' — in the sense of having 'woken up to reality.' Siddhartha Gautama was born in Nepal around 2,500 years ago. He did not claim to be a god or a prophet. He was a human who became enlightened, understanding life in the deepest way possible. Blend contains sandalwood, myrrh, frankincense, and other herbs and essential oils in a base of fractionated coconut oil.

Candle color = white
Psalm = 85

MONEY DRAWING - St. Martin of Tours

Money Drawing oil is used to bring money, good fortune, jobs and lucrative dealings into your life. St. Martin of Tours is often venerated as a military saint. One often told story claims that he cut his cloak in half and gave one-half to a beggar. In a dream, he saw the beggar as Jesus, sporting half his cloak. When he awoke, he found his cloak restored to its whole state. Blend contains cinnamon, patchouli, ginger, and other herbs and essential oils in a base of fractionated coconut oil.

Petition St. Martin of Tours to draw money to you, to bring customers into your business, and to bring luck and good fortune.

Candle color = green
Psalm = 119 v. 17-24

PEACE - Our Lady of Guadalupe

Peace oil is used to bring peace and tranquility into your life, and promote a harmonious existence with nature. It can also be used to end disputes and reconcile friendships. Our Lady of Guadalupe, also known as the Virgin of Guadalupe, is also venerated by Native Americans. Blend contains tangerine, ylang-ylang, lavender buds, and other herbs and essential oils in a base of fractionated coconut oil.

Petition Our Lady of Guadalupe to request peace in times of turmoil and stress, to assist with healing the sick, and for assistance in spiritual guidance.

Candle color = pink
Psalm = 39

PERSONAL POWER - St. Joan of Arc

Personal Power oil is used to boost confidence, instill courage and bravery, and promote a love of self. This oil helps activate the Solar Plexus Chakra to build inner strength. Joan of Arc is considered a heroine of France for her role during the Lancastrian phase of the Hundred Years' War, and was canonized as a Roman Catholic saint. She was only 13 when she began to hear voices of Archangel Michael, and then those of St. Catherine and St. Margaret, telling her to rescue France. She was burned at the stake in 1431. She is associated with honor, power, and courage and is nicknamed 'the maid of Orleans.' Blend contains verbena, cajeput, John the Conqueror, and other herbs and essential oils in a base of fractionated coconut oil.

Petition St. Joan of Arc for courage and strength, for assistance to defeat your enemies, and for freedom from restrictions.

Candle color = yellow
Psalm = 39

PROTECTION - St. Christopher

Protection oil is used to protect yourself, your loved ones, and your property from harm and negative intentions. Use this oil to keep your enemies away. St. Christopher is one of the most popular Catholic figures. Many consider him a saint, although he is only considered a martyr in the Roman Catholic church. Christopher is said to mean 'christ bearer.'

Petition St. Christopher for protection from enemies, accidents, storms and death, and to reach your destination safely when traveling. Blend contains clove, agrimony, black pepper, and other herbs and essential oils in a base of fractionated coconut oil.

Candle color = purple
Psalm = 1

PSYCHIC VISION - St. Gerard Majella

Psychic Vision oil is used to develop or enhance your psychic visions during card or rune readings, divination, and energy healing. Gerard Majella is honored as a saint in the Roman Catholic Church. His blessings are often sought for unborn children, mothers, and people falsely accused of crimes. He shared stories of his prophetic dreams which were reported to have come true. Blend contains anise, bearberry, mugwort, and other herbs and essential oils in a base of fractionated coconut oil.

Petition St. Gerard Majella for psychic vision, channeling and mediumship work; for expectant mothers, and for fertility problems.

Candle color = violet
Psalm = 78

PURIFICATION - St. Therese of Lisieux

Purification oil is used to cleanse the mind, spirit, and aura of all negativity. This blend can be used before ritual or ceremonial work as well. Saint Thérèse of Lisieux was a Roman Catholic French Discalced Carmelite nun widely venerated in modern times. Some call St. Therese of Lisieux the "The Little Flower of Jesus." Although she never went on one, she is the patron saint of the missions because of her love for their good deeds. Blend contains lemongrass, tea tree, rosemary, sea salt, and other herbs and essential oils in a base of fractionated coconut oil.

Petition St. Therese of Lisieux for protection from those who mean us harm, to help restore our faith in ourselves and others, to assist us in showing love and compassion, and for assistance in abandoning negative patterns such as addiction and self-harm.

Candle color = white
Psalm = 119 v. 9-16

REIKI - Mother Teresa

Reiki oil is used to enhance Reiki energy during and after treatments to promote healing. This oil can assist Reiki practitioners and recipients. It can also be used for global healing. Reiki is a form of alternative healing discovered by a Japanese Buddhist monk named Mikao Usui. Reiki is now used in many cultural traditions across the world. Reiki practitioners use a technique through which a "universal energy" is said to transfer energy from the palms of the healer to the client to encourage emotional or physical healing. Mother Teresa is known in the Catholic Church as Saint Teresa of Calcutta. She was an Albanian-Indian Roman Catholic nun and missionary. She worked on many missions throughout her life, serving the poor and ill and opened many houses that catered to the needs of AIDS patients. Blend contains orange, eucalyptus, lemon balm, and other herbs and essential oils in a base of fractionated coconut oil.

Candle color = blue
Psalm = 102

THUNDERBIRD

SHAMAN BLESSINGS
SPIRIT ESSENTIALS

SHAMAN BLESSINGS - Thunderbird

Shaman Blessing oil is used to bless people, sacred space, altars and property. This is a great oil to use before and during rituals, altar work, and initiations. A shaman is a person known to walk between both worlds and commune with spirits in order to provide divination and healing. Native Americans view the Thunderbird as a symbol of the separation between the heavens and the earth. In some Native American traditions, the Thunderbird is seen with the sun as its eyes – open and bright in the daytime, closed at night to bring on the darkness. Blend contains cedarwood, sage, sweetgrass, and other herbs and essential oils in a base of fractionated coconut oil.

Candle color = white
Psalm = 62

SUCCESS - St. Peter

Success oil is used to bring success to your life and dealings. Use this oil to be a success at work, in business ventures, artistic work, lifestyle changes, and to help curb addictions. In the New Testament, Peter was one of the twelve Apostles of Jesus Christ. Roman Catholics view Peter as the first pope and leader of the Christian Church. Blend contains wintergreen, High John, ginger, and other herbs and essential oils in a base of fractionated coconut oil.

Petition St. Peter for success in business and new ventures, for good fortune, to remove difficulties in meeting your goals, and for endurance and strength.

Candle color = green or blue

UNHEXING - St. Cyprian

Unhexing oil is used to remove curses, jinxes, and hexes placed on you by your enemies and those who mean you harm. For added strength, use with a reversing candle. Born to a high-ranking pagan family in Roman Africa, probably during 200-210 AD, Cyprian was converted to Christianity about 246 AD. It is said that he turned to the church after all of his magical attempts to persuade his true love failed. This places him between the worlds of his magical Pagan roots and his newfound dedication to Christianity. He was a prolific writer of church documents and when the Anglican church broke free from the Roman Catholic church, many of Cyprian's documents were used to support their movement. He is the unofficial saint of sorcerers.

Petition St. Cyprian to protect you and your loved ones from harm due to baneful magic; to protect your reputation from liars and rumors; from those that harass you; and from annoying neighbors. Blend contains citronella, agrimony, juniper berry, and other herbs and essential oils in a base of fractionated coconut oil.

Candle color = gray
Psalm = 7

ROOT CHAKRA - Archangel Uriel

Root Chakra oil is used to activate and balance the root chakra. The root chakra is the foundation of life. It affects security, sensuality, stability, and sexuality. Archangel Uriel is considered the angel of wisdom and is said to shine the light truth into the darkness of confusion. Uriel is considered a Prince of the Presence, which is an angel who is allowed to enter the presence of God. Uriel means "God is my light." Blend contains clove, frankincense, black pepper, and other herbs and essential oils in a base of fractionated coconut oil.

Archangel Uriel oil is a blend designed for those who need to create a more grounded and stable life. It helps those who feel they have lost their foundation and meaning in life. It is used to increase your life force by releasing deep energy blocks and feelings of loneliness and abandonment.

Element = earth
Candle color = red
Psalm = 106

SACRAL CHAKRA - Archangel Gabriel

Sacral Chakra oil is used to activate and balance the sacral chakra. The sacral chakra is associated with creativity and joy. It affects reproduction, creativity, joy, and enthusiasm. In the Abrahamic religions, Gabriel is an angel who serves as a messenger for God. He is the angel who appeared to Mary, telling the birth of Jesus. Blend contains clary sage, spearmint, burdock, hops, and other herbs and essential oils in a base of fractionated coconut oil.

Archangel Gabriel oil is designed for those who need to discover their unique identity and creativity, which leads to happiness and fulfillment through originality and a positive outlook on life. Grief, loss, and life transitions.

Element = water
Candle color = orange
Psalm = 47

SOLAR PLEXUS CHAKRA - Archangel Jophiel

Solar Plexus Chakra oil is used to activate and balance the solar plexus chakra. The solar plexus chakra is associated with emotions and confidence. It affects digestion, power, personal growth, and ego. Archangel Jophiel is the angel of wisdom and understanding. Archangel Jophiel is considered the keeper of the Torah and all wisdom, and an angel of the seventh heaven. Some scholars show him as the angel in charge of the cherubim. Blend contains grapefruit, mandarin, fennel, rosemary, and other herbs and essential oils in a base of fractionated coconut oil.

Archangel Jophiel oil designed for those who need assistance with power and ego struggles, self-confidence issues, and manifesting goals. It helps align your purpose with your higher-self, increases self-control, improves self-esteem, assists with concentration, and can help recover soul fragments for those who have experienced deep trauma.

Element = fire
Candle color = yellow
Psalm = 71

HEART CHAKRA - Archangel Raphael

Heart Chakra oil is used to activate and balance the heart chakra. The heart chakra is where unconditional love and compassion develops. It affects circulation, passion, love, and devotion. Archangel Raphael is known for performing all manners of healing in Judaic, Christian, and Islamic traditions. Archangel Raphael is claimed by many to be the patron saint of travelers, the blind, nurses, physicians, medical workers, matchmakers, and Christian marriage. Blend contains lavender, palmarosa, thyme, and other herbs and essential oils in a base of fractionated coconut oil.

Archangel Raphael oil is designed those who need to learn and accept unconditional love for themselves and others. It assists with healing work, balancing physical and mental energies, understanding childhood memories, relieving feelings of anxiety and stress, setting boundaries, and lessening feelings of restrictions.

Element = air
Candle color = green
Psalm = 47

THROAT CHAKRA - Archangel Michael

Throat Chakra oil is used to activate and balance the throat chakra. The throat chakra affects all communication, fluent thought, independence, and inspiration. Archangel Michael is the patron saint of warriors, although the ill and suffering also claim him as their patron. Blend contains eucalyptus, orange, lemon balm, and other herbs and essential oils in a base of fractionated coconut oil.

Archangel Michael oil is designed for those who need assistance communicating with themselves and others. It helps alleviate the fear of speaking your own truth, and removing you from situations that are not in alignment with your truth; let go of fear and self-doubt, and cut emotional ties.

Element = ether
Candle color = light blue
Psalm = 45

THIRD EYE CHAKRA - Archangel Raziel

Third Eye Chakra oil is used to activate and balance the third eye chakra. The third eye chakra represents the inner eye and duality. It affects visualization, intuition, clarity, and meditation. Archangel Raziel is known as the "Keeper of Secrets, " and the "Angel of Mysteries," The Book of Raziel is said to be a magical book containing all secret knowledge, created by Raziel who stays close to God's throne, recording all things discussed. Blend contains sandalwood, star anise, bearberry, and other herbs and essential oils in a base of fractionated coconut oil.

Archangel Raziel oil is designed to create a mystical balance in your life by clarifying your natural senses of intuition, clairvoyance, clairaudience, and clairsentience.

Element = avyakta
Candle color = dark blue
Psalm = 49

CROWN CHAKRA - Archangel Zadkiel

Crown Chakra oil is used to activate and balance the crown chakra. The crown chakra opens us to higher consciousness. It affects meditation, universal consciousness, beingness, and unity. It puts us in touch with the "I AM" consciousness. Zadkiel means "Righteousness of God" or "Grace of God" and is the archangel of freedom, benevolence, mercy, and forgiveness. Zadkiel is sometimes referred to as the angel of mercy. Zadkiel is one of two who follows directly behind Michael as the head archangel enters battle. Blend contains frankincense, rosemary, marshmallow, and other herbs and essential oils in a base of fractionated coconut oil.

Archangel Zadkiel oil is designed to open your cosmic awareness and help lift you to the cosmic consciousness. It can assist with overcoming addictions, past life regression, deeper meditations, and emotional calming.

Element = cosmic energy
Candle color = violet or white
Psalm = 14

SOUL CHAKRA - Archangel Metatron

Soul Chakra oil is used to activate and balance the soul chakra. The soul chakra is known as the 'seat of the soul.' It initiates enlightenment, and aides in light body activation. Metatron is an archangel known in Judaism as the Recording Angel or the Chancellor of Heaven. Archangel Metatron uses the Merkabah cube for healing and clearing away lower energies. Blend contains cedarwood, geranium, nutmeg, and other herbs and essential oils in a base of fractionated coconut oil.

Archangel Metatron oil is designed to clear emotional debris, cleanse emotions, bring inner peace, and can assist in times of life transformation by cleaning the slate of emotional baggage.

Candle color = white or gold
Psalm = 25

ANGEL CHAKRA - Archangel Tzaphkiel

The Angel Chakra, also known as the 5th Eye Chakra, is located at the top of the head. When fully activated, it allows you to easily communicate with your angels on a daily basis. Archangel Tzaphkiel is the angel of deep contemplation of God and represents the divine feminine in the creation stories. She increases insight, mysticism, and discernment by helping to develop the feminine side of your being. Blend contains grapefruit, sandalwood, dandelion, peppermint and other herbs and essential oils in a base of fractionated coconut oil.

Archangel Tzaphkiel oil is designed to open your

communication with angelic beings. It can assist you obtaining a deeper contemplation of God, and assist with entering the deep mysteries of the divine feminine.

Candle color = white
Psalm = 23

BALANCE - 4TH EYE CHAKRA - Archangel Auriel

The 4th Eye Chakra is located on the forehead just above the Brow Chakra. It works with the lunar energies to balance the fluid functions of the body and helps you use your intuition and examine your feelings.

Archangel Auriel is known as the Angel of Destiny. She is a moon angel who helps us understand the unconscious mind. Invoke Archangel Auriel when you want to increase your natural intuition, work with the moon energy for spells, and to restore balance in your physical and mental lives. Blend contains lemon, palmarosa, thyme and other herbs and essential oils in a base of fractionated coconut oil.

Candle color = purple

EARTH CHAKRA - Archangel Sandalphon

The Earth Chakra is located about 12 inches below the feet. It increases prana life force, integrates healing energy into the physical body, and heals the Earth. This chakra unifies the whole self by releasing the energy of alienation. Shamans use this energy for healing. Blend contains ginger, thyme, nutmeg and other herbs and essential oils in a base of fractionated coconut oil.

Archangel Sandalphon is known as the Keeper of the Earth. Sandalphon is the divine twin of Metatron, and together they are the Alpha and Omega. Working with

Sandalphon is to have respect for all life and the Earth. Invoke Archangel Sandalphon to aid your immune system, to stay grounded during spiritual practices, to assist you on a shamanic path, and to assist you in finding the core cause of a problem. Archangel Sandalphon is often called upon to determine the gender of a child before and during conception.

Candle color = brown or other earth colors

RELATIONSHIP - CHRIST CONSCIOUSNESS - Archangel Chamuel

Archangel Chamuel aids us in deepening our relationships and can guide you through life changing situations such as divorce, conflict, grief, and job loss. Archangel Chamuel also helps improve loving relationships with others by developing the compassionate side of the heart chakra. As your compassion grows, Archangel Chamuel oil can be used to help you receive the Christ-Consciousness. Blend contains bergamot, verbena, sage and other herbs and essential oils in a base of fractionated coconut oil.

Petition Archangel Chamuel to increase your inner happiness, to open your heart chakra for living in a state of gratitude, to assist in attracting your soulmate, and to physically and emotionally heal the parts of your body and life you have rejected.

Candle color = pink

OILS AND PSYCHIC ANOINTMENTS

INDIAN GUIDE

MAGNET Magnet

● HERE IS OUR Complete LIST OILS

☐ Magnet Oil
☐ Commanding Oil
☐ Altar Oil
☐ Lucky Plant Oil
☐ Black Art Oil
☐ Buddha Oil
☐ High Conquering Oil
☐ Incense Oil
☐ Spirit Oil
☐ Lover's Oil
☐ Attraction Oil
☐ Crucifixion Oil
☐ Holy Bath Oil
☐ Concentration Oil
☐ Cleopatra Oil

☐ Hindu Grass Oil
☐ Power Oil
☐ Exodus Oil
☐ Success Oil
☐ 7th Heaven Oil
☐ King Solomon Oil
☐ 5 Circles Oil
☐ Dove's Blood Oil
☐ Angel Oil
☐ Compelling Oil
☐ Indian Guide Oil
☐ Temple Oil
☐ Chinese Oil
☐ Bat's Blood Oil
☐ Bible Bouquet Oil

50c EACH ● YOUR SELECTION OF ANY 3 OILS FOR . . . $1 25

The names used in connection with these oils or perfumes are not to be construed as indicative of any use or guarantee in connection with them. These names merely denote the impression that the author had received from their fragrance and the thoughts that they evoke in his mind. We do, however, guarantee that these oils and perfumes are of an excellent quality, purity, and strength, selected with skill and care and offered to you as being of the best value.

WORKING MAGIC WITH OILS IN SPELLS, RITUALS, AND PRAYERS

Probably the most important of all ingredients found in a magical oil is your intention. Purpose, faith, focus, and emotion set magical waves in motion. It is something I preach about often to clients - that no oil, candle, powder, or herb will do you any good without putting something of yourself into the work. Rubbing oil on a candle, lighting it, and walking away will not bring you what you want. When I create a batch of oils, I pray over them, asking that they work for whoever receives them. If the oil is of a loving nature, I imagine loving thoughts and request that they enter the bottle. For a money blend, I concentrate on rolls of cash, stacks of coins, and bills being marked 'paid' and ask all Guides and Gods to help make it so.

When you use an oil created with this type of focus then combine it with your own, it is like having two practitioners working on your situation. Several years ago, we began burning 'money drawing' candles in the shop daily. Within a few months of starting it, sales began to pick up and have continued to grow ever since. Every time we look up and see that lit candle (dressed with our oil, of course) it aligns our focus on keeping a store that is clean, well-stocked, friendly, and exciting. That intention creates an atmosphere for the customers, which creates more business. Because, when all is said and done, this is what magic is, what spellwork is — directing all your energy towards the desired goal.

Before we dive into the spells section, I wanted to take a little time to go over the types of candles most often used as well as their color associations. The size of the candles mentioned in the spells section can easily be changed out for a larger or smaller size, depending on the length of time you want the work to last.

Spell Candle - 4 inches tall and 1/2-inch-thick, they are often called a 'chime candle.' New Age shops have been selling these for years. They are affordable, usually under fifty cents each, and burn for approximately 2 to 3 hours. If kept out of drafts, these candles usually burn away to almost nothing without leftover wax.

Offertory Candle - 6 inches tall and 3/4 inches thick, some people refer to these as 'household candles' because they are the same size as those used in emergencies when the electricity is out. The burn time is around 5 to 7 hours.

Jumbo Pillar Candle - 9 inches tall and 1.5 inches thick, these candles are great for ritual use. They are large enough to carve sigils, petitions, and prayers into the wax. Burn time is about 30 hours.

Vigil Candles - encased in glass and 8 inches tall. Here, things get a little tricky because some religions and paths (and shops) use the term 'vigil' to mean a smaller candle. We are using the term most often used in botanicas, witchcraft, and Hoodoo shops which are also known as 7-day candles. Do they truly burn seven days?   Not always. The usual burn time is between five and seven days, depending on the manufacturer of the candle and the conditions it is burned in.

Figural Candles - sometimes called 'image candles,' these are candles that are in the shape of specific objects or people. You can find them in male, female, couples, cats, crosses, skulls, and more. They provide a strong focus on an individual or situation and are usually large enough for you to carve your intentions onto the surface. Their visual symbolism can help to create very specific spells.

Choosing Colors in Magical Work

Here, we go over the colors of candles. But, you can take this chart a step further and use it to select altar fabrics, colors of sewn dolls, mojo bags, or petitions made from colored paper. Each color is said to have its own magical purposes, its individual vibration. The symbolism and associations of colors vary according to magical traditions, religion, or culture but you will find that many have the same meanings across the globe. Before the creation of colored candles, white candles were used for almost every form of magical work, which is one reason why they are still used today as a "stand-in" for any other color.

CANDLE COLOR ASSOCIATIONS

- white -- truth, purity, healing, blessings
- blue -- peace, healing, good intentions, changeability
- green -- money spells, business, abundance, career
- yellow -- friendship, prayer, happiness, attraction, wisdom
- red -- love spells, passion, fertility, physical strength, potency
- pink -- devotion, romance, emotional healing, partnership, honor
- purple -- power, ambition, psychic powers, commanding, recognition, expansion
- orange -- creativity, road opening, self-confidence, career, legal matters
- brown -- court case spells, legal difficulties, concentration, telepathy
- black – banishing, negativity, crossing, uncrossing, discord, evil
- red and black (Reversing) -- remove a hex hindering love or passion
- white and black (Reversing) – from bad to good, return a spell to the one who cast it
- green and black (Reversing) – remove a jinx that hinders financial success

SPELLS OF LOVE, ATTRACTION, AND RECONCILIATION

Here you will find spells and magical workings of all types. But remember, a spell doesn't have to be elaborate or complicated to be effective. With the proper ingredients and the right emotion behind it, a simple candle altar burning can work wonders. Also, if you carefully read all the magical oil descriptions, you will find many other spell methods, tricks, and useful spell casting information.

MOVING CANDLE COME TO ME SPELL –

this is to bring someone closer to you, perhaps someone you have an interest in, but the "spark" hasn't quite happened yet. This same work can be used for a spell of reconciliation. If that is the case, just replace the COME TO ME oil with RECONCILE oil and write your petition accordingly. This spell calls for a male and a female figural candle. Replace, if needed, according to your sexual orientation.

- What you will need:
- 1 male figural candle, red or pink

- 1 female figural candle, red or pink
- COME TO ME oil
- rose petals
- 1 lodestone
- paper and pencil
- red or pink ribbon

First, carve the names for each person on the candle that represents them. For the male, write his name and on the female, her name. If you don't want to use a knife, you can easily carve words into the candle using the tip of an ink pen or even a toothpick. Rub COME TO ME oil into each candle over your carvings in an upward motion. If you happen to have hair from the person you want to attract, place it under their candle. You can do the same with your own.

These candles will melt and run across a surface. You need something flat with a lip around the edges to place the candles on. A cookie sheet lined with aluminum foil makes for a simple, easy to clean up workspace. Write your name on a piece of paper seven times. Now, turn the paper and write your love interest's name seven times so that it interlocks with your name. This will "weave" the two names together. Anoint each corner and the center of the paper with your COME TO ME oil. Place the petition paper in the center of the cookie sheet and set the lodestone on top of it.

Now, set each candle on opposite sides of the cookie sheet facing each other. It isn't necessary to move them all the way to each edge. You want to leave enough room around the sheet so that you can sprinkle a ring of rose petals all the way around the two candles, locking them into a circle of roses.

Light each candle, and state your intention. The wording doesn't have to be lengthy or rhyme. Simply speak from the heart and say what you want to happen. Some people choose to pray at this time. Every 10 minutes scoot each candle a little closer to the center, about an inch or so. After doing this several times, the candles should be touching (or almost touching, depending on how to candle is made) and both be on top of your petition paper. Now that they have moved across the surface and finally found each other, allow them to burn the rest of the way down without disturbing. The next day, gather the rose petals from the surface. You can either save them to use in a mojo bag later or sprinkle a few petals into your bath water on the days you plan to see your intended. Also, keep a little COME TO ME oil behind your ears or on your wrists when you know the two of you will be together. Gather the foil around the wax and tie with a red or pink ribbon. Place under your bed for seven nights. After the seven days is up, bury in your front yard beside the porch to entice them to come to your house. If you live in an apartment, you can bury at the bottom of a potted plant. I knew someone who placed it in the bottom of the umbrella stand beside her front door.

GET OVER A LOVE GONE BAD –

this spell is to release the emotions you have for someone so that you can get past the pain and move forward. For cutting out the sting of a bad breakup or when someone never returned your feelings, it is time to cut things loose and clear the path for a bright future.

- What you will need:
- 1 peony root
- 1 piece of Queen Elizabeth root
- CUT AND CLEAR oil

- 1 black bag or square of fabric
- black thread
- photo of the person you want to get over
- 1 banana peel

Take a pen with black ink and cover the face in the picture with rows and rows of X's – all the way across the picture, line after line until the entire surface is covered. With each X made, you know that you are canceling out your connection to this person. Take the piece of Queen Elizabeth root and place it under your tongue and say something to the effect of, "you no longer influence me. I cut away all emotional connection we had." Then, spit the piece of Queen Elizabeth root into the center of the picture. Fold the picture three times away from you.

Next, anoint the peony root with the CUT AND CLEAR oil. Place the peony root on the center of the folded picture and fold it one more time, the opposite direction of your first folds (long ways) but still making sure to fold away from you, not towards. Take the black thread and begin winding it around the picture (moving away from you while wrapping) with both roots trapped inside until you have fully bound everything in a cage of black thread.

Place into the black bag or tie into the square of black cloth. Wrap the banana peel tightly around the bag and bury in the farthest corner of your yard. The peel will encourage worms to eat away at it and as the bag deteriorates, so will your connection to this person.

REPAIR A MARRIAGE SPELL –

this is for a couple that is still together, but things have either become stale, strained or distant. The reason I mention that the couple should still be together is that this is a spell to strengthen and repair. If the couple were already separated, then a spell of reconciliation would be needed instead.

- What you will need:
- 1 white spell candle
- 1 pink spell candle
- ADAM AND EVE oil
- Piece of thin wire, about 6 to 8 inches long (beading wire works well)
- 2 spell candle holders
- picture of the two of you together

On the picture, front and back, write out all the things that attracted you to each other in the first place. You can mention things you like to do together, things in common, things that make you laugh, good memories –anything positive about the relationship. Be as detailed as you like. If you run out of space, write on top of the words you have already written. When you have finished writing, your mind should be in a happy place, thinking about all the great times and the high points of your union. Anoint the picture in the sign of the cross with the ADAM AND EVE oil with a dab at the top, bottom, left, and right. Add one more in the center of the picture then fold it towards you twice. Set out your candle holders and place the photo beneath them.

Next, choose one candle to represent you and the other for your spouse. Write your names on the candle that stands for each of you then anoint the candles with a little of the ADAM AND EVE oil, rubbing the oil with an upwards motion. Take one of the candles and place it in the candleholder. Now get your wire and curl one end around the candle. Place the other candle in the next holder and wrap the other end of the wire around the second candle. They should now be joined by the wire. Light the candles and allow them to burn until they are gone.

When they have finished, place the photo between the mattresses or tie to the bottom of the bed. Take the wire that bound the candles and wind it around the foot of the bedpost towards the head of the bed on the side your spouse sleeps. If possible, plan a night of romance in that same bed.

MAKE A LOVER STOP WANDERING –

this is a very traditional Hoodoo spell to make your wandering lover (or spouse) want to return home and stay there with you. Take their left shoe and anoint the bottom of the shoes with RETURN TO ME oil, mainly towards the front of the shoe where the toes would be. Sift together equal parts of salt and pepper and drop them into the shoe. Stand at the front door and point the shoe inside (toes towards the inside of the house). Shake the salt and pepper inside the shoe as you walk towards the back door. Dump the contents out the back door. Salt and pepper the shoe two more times until you have performed this three times total, each time pointing into the house and shake out the contents out the back door. When you have finished, place both shoes back where you found them but make sure to point them in the same direction as if the person were walking into the front door. Finally, dress the threshold of the front door with your RETURN TO ME oil.

LOVE ATTRACTING DOUBLE MOJO –

this mojo bag is to help the right love to find you.

- What you will need:
- Small square blue fabric (preferably silk, about 3 x 3 inches)
- Blue thread
- a snippet of your hair
- LOVE ATTRACTING or ARCHANGEL ANAEL oil
- lavender buds
- a coffee bean
- red flannel square of fabric (about 5 x 5 inches)
- twine or red thread

If you are feeling apprehension about cutting your hair, it doesn't have to be a long, noticeable strand. It can even be snippets from the ends. Gather this hair in the center of the blue cloth and gather up into a little pouch. Begin to wind the blue thread around the neck of the cloth where it gathers together, making sure to wind facing towards you. When you have finished, tie off and anoint the bag with the love oil.

Now take the square of red flannel and place in the middle of it: the coffee bean, a pinch of lavender buds, and the small blue mojo bag. Gather up just as you did the first bag and tie it off, once again winding towards you. Your blue bag containing your hair and the love oil should now be encased in the red flannel mojo with the other ingredients. Sleep with the double mojo bag for three nights in a row and carry with you whenever you go out in public. Is said to draw the attraction of true love.

SPELLS OF PROTECTION

CROSS OF MICHAEL –

this spell is not only one of protection, but also for creating a protective amulet that you will wear on your body.

- What you will need:
- 4 white spell or taper candles
- St. Michael medallion
- 4 quartz crystals
- red brick dust
- WALL OF FIRE Protection oil
- ARCHANGEL MICHAEL oil

Place the white candles in the sign of the cross - top, bottom, left and right and anoint each one with WALL OF FIRE.

Now anoint your four quartz crystals with the WALL OF FIRE oil and place in the empty spaces between the candles. Next, anoint the St. Michael medallion with the oil and place in the center of the candles. Rub the palm of your hand with the ARCHANGEL MICHAEL oil then pour a little red brick dust on top of it. Gently blow across the entire work surface, allowing the dust to settle on the candles, the medallion, and the crystals.

Light the candles and say this prayer to St. Michael

Holy Michael, the Archangel, defend us in battle. Be our safeguard against the wickedness and snares of the devil. May God rebuke him, we humbly pray, and do you, O Prince of the heavenly host, by the power of God cast into hell Satan and all the evil spirits who wander through the world seeking the ruin of souls. Amen.

When the candles have finished burning, you wear the medallion as an amulet of protection and place the four crystals at the four corners of your house which will act of Talismans of Protection.

FIRE AND SALT PROTECTION BOTTLE –

easy to put together but packs a powerful punch. Combines the elements of protection found in both witchcraft and Hoodoo.

- What you will need:
- small glass bottle with cork or lid
- bay leaf
- clove garlic
- salt
- sage
- 2 red spell candles
- WALL OF FIRE or SAINT CHRISTOPHER oil

Choose a bottle that is small enough to hide under your front porch or bury near (if you have a porch that can't be accessed underneath.) Pour about two capfuls of protection oil inside the bottle. Put inside: the bay leaf, sage, and clove of garlic. If the neck of the bottle is too small, feel free to chop up the garlic clove and stuff into the bottle. Top off with salt, filling to the top and cork tightly. Anoint the two red spell candles with the anointing oil and burn on either side of the bottle, while saying a prayer for protection. A simple biblical protection passage is found in Psalms 59:1 Deliver me from my enemies, O God; be my fortress against those who are attacking me. When the candles have completely burned away, place the bottle under your front porch or bury beside it.

PROTECTION EGGSHELL POWDER –

plan ahead for keeping protection powder in your home by saving your eggshells. If you are in a hurry, break three eggs and thoroughly rinse out the shells. It is much easier to clean the shells if you do it immediately after cracking. Allow to dry thoroughly. For faster drying, place on a cookie sheet and place in oven on lowest setting for five minutes or so. This is a protection power that you can use in many ways: spread around your property, blow across protection candles, sprinkle under the welcome mat, as a mojo bag ingredient, etc. There are many possibilities.

- What you will need:
- 3 egg shells
- 1 teaspoon powdered ginger
- 1 teaspoon sage
- 4 tablespoons cornstarch
- PROTECT ME oil

First, place the cornstarch in a glass bowl and add about a half capful of PROTECT ME oil. To incorporate the oil with the powder, mix well with your fingers then begin the rub the powder between your hands over the bowl. This rubbing action will help to spread the oil throughout all of the powder. When completely mixed, add powdered ginger and sage and mix well again. Now, when your egg shells are completely dry and cool (if you dried in the oven), you begin to break them up. Using a mortar and pestle is suitable for pulverizing the shells into smaller fragments. Some people keep a coffee grinder just for magical purposes which will turn the shells into a powder. When you have crushed the eggshells as small as you can, add to your batch of ingredients and mix again. The oil in the mixture may still be a bit moist so spread out the powder flat and allow to dry well overnight. Bag or place in a glass jar for future use.

SPELLS OF POWER

PYRAMID OF POWER –

this spell is one of personal power, to regain your confidence and take back control of all your good qualities so that you can forge the life you want to create.

- What you will need:
- 1 purple vigil candle
- 1 black vigil candle
- 1 white vigil candle
- JOAN OF ARC oil
- JINX BEGONE or SAINT CYPRIAN oil
- BLESSING oil

Take three vigil candles: one purple, one black, and one white. Form in a triangle with the purple candle at the head, the black to the bottom left, and the white to the right left. Purple candle, dress with JOAN OF ARC oil; Black candle, dress with JINX BEGONE or SAINT CYPRIAN oil; White candle, dress with BLESSING oil.

In the center of these three candles, place a small bowl of sugar and put a picture of yourself in the bowl. If you can, try to choose a picture of yourself that you genuinely like, one that was taken on a happy day. On the back of the picture, write out all of your good qualities and things that make you feel blessed. Anoint in the sign of the cross with the BLESSING OIL.

To the left of the black candle, place a fire safe dish. Write out all things that are holding you back in life such as bad habits, certain people, or unpleasant situations. Each day, until all the candles have burned out, tear the paper into smaller pieces and move further away from the candles. When all the candles have finished burning, burn the pieces of paper. Take the ashes outside at sunset and blow them to the West in the direction of the setting sun.

Take your photograph, fold it towards you three times and carry with for the next three weeks. Longer if you prefer and can use it as an ingredient in a mojo bag.

CROWN OF ACHIEVEMENT SPELL –

sometimes you will find this as 'crown of success' and is meant to help in spells for succeeding in life and achieving your goals. Said to be especially influential for artists, singers, songwriters, writers, or those who make their living by creating this with their hands. However, it can just as easily be used by anyone who seeks to increase their mastery.

- What you will need:
- 7 purple spell candles
- CROWN OF ACHIEVEMENT oil
- a silver needle
- picture or photocopy of a crown

This spell is to be performed for 7 days. The time of day is unimportant, as long as one candle per day is burned. First, you will write out your wish or petition on the picture of the crown. Allow the words you use to follow the outline of the crown, its inside lines and the base. The point is to make your words become the crown. In other words, if it were possible to erase the picture of the crown, your words left behind would still create the outline of a crown. Don't get too obsessed with the artistry of it – just write on the lines and focus your intention. Anoint the four corners of the paper with the CROWN oil and set aside.

Take the needle and carve the words 'success' and your name into each of the seven candles while thinking of your goal. Anoint each candle in an upwards motion with the CROWN OF ACHIEVEMENT oil. When you are ready to begin day one of your seven-day spell, place the crown petition under the candle holder and light the first candle and allow to burn completely until finished. With all of your candle already carved and anointed, on the following days, you only have to state your intention again before lighting the next candle. When the seven days are finished, and all candles have burned, get a fire-safe dish of some sort (like a cauldron or ashtray) and burn your petition. Take outside and blow the ashes to the East, the direction of the sunrise.

SPELLS OF MONEY AND SUCCESS

MONEY DRAWING HONEY JAR –

in our store we have a money drawing honey jar that all of us have contributed to. Inside, we have each taken a piece of our personal business cards and written on them our individual petitions for money and success. Honey jars are meant to "sweeten" your situation.

- What you will need:
- 4-ounce jelly jar (1/2 pint if you want a larger one) with lid
- cinnamon sticks
- fenugreek seeds
- alfalfa
- 1 lodestone
- 1 piece pyrite
- a coin
- honey
- MONEY DRAWING or SAINT MARTIN OF TOURS oil
- petition paper or business card
- green spell candles

I always choose a unique coin, one that seems like a sacrifice to give up such as a silver dollar. My personal money drawing jar contains a Sacagawea dollar. Some people prefer to add three silver dimes. Place money, 1 to 3 cinnamon sticks, lodestone, and pyrite into the jar. Add a pinch of dried alfalfa and a pinch of fenugreek seeds.

Prepare your petition using a business card or a small piece of paper. State your level of success you wish to achieve. I usually cover the card in dollar signs, front and back on top of my petition. Fold towards you and place into jar. Fill the jar with honey almost to the top but leave a little room. Taste the honey and state your petition out loud, speaking it into the jar. Add a capful of money oil to the jar and screw on lid. From here on out, you can burn green candles on top of the jar to keep the money drawing energy flowing.

MONEY DRAWING ANOINTING –

I wanted to share with you some of the ways to use money drawing oil. For starters, use it on items that actually represent money. Take a small amount and rub on wallets and purses is an excellent use of the oil. Wearing on the hands during a job interview is another money magic trick. However, be sure to use only a small amount. The smell of cinnamon is strong, so you don't want to overpower your meeting with its scent or leave an oily residue when you shake someone's hand. It being present on your hands is the important things – not the quantity.

Use on paperwork that deals with money matters. Anoint your bank statements on top, bottom, left, and right with the oil and add a zero to your bank balance. Some people use a bank record as the paper for writing out a long letter of petition, stating future plans for money and finances. You can also use to anoint tax returns - only YOUR copy of the return – do NOT send an herbal anointed tax return to the IRS or you may find yourself under investigation. Once, a client went overboard with sprinkling money drawing powder on her cash. The bank interrogated her over it, concerned about the white powder. Alternatively, if you file your taxes electronically, have money drawing oil on your fingertips while typing.

If you make your living by creating things with your hands, keep money drawing oil on them while you work to increase your success.

If your finances are in a comfortable place, but you need help on saving more or managing your money better, use some of the same tricks above and use the MONEY LASTS oil. You can always mix MONEY DRAWING, or SAINT MARTIN OF TOURS with MONEY LASTS so that your money increases and works better for you. If you can find a statue of St. Martin of Tours, keep him in your home to allow the money to continue to flow into your household and anoint him with his own oil.

MONEY DRAWING VIGIL CANDLE –

we keep one of these burning in our store whenever the shop is open. There have been a few times when business was exceptionally slow, and we discovered that the candle hadn't been lit yet. Lighting it always seems to improve the flow of customers.

- What you will need:
- 1 green 7-day glass candle
- MONEY DRAWING oil
- powdered cinnamon

One thing that we enjoy in creating 7-day candles for our own use is finding interesting pictures for a label. If you don't intend to resell the candle, you have the artistic freedom to use almost any picture on the internet that symbolizes your goal. However, it is best to stay away from actual candle labels that other magical houses have produced if you are going to be burning it for the public eye. It would be considered in poor taste to represent that your candle came from one of these companies when it did not. An excellent label is to tape an actual dollar bill right on the jar. Magically speaking, a two-dollar bill would be preferred. I use shipping tape to do this, and it creates a protective barrier. You can easily reuse by cutting the tape around the bill to release it – the tape again and use on your next candle. You also have the option of leaving the glass plain if you don't want others to notice your spellwork. For secretive purposes, cover the glass with dollar signs in chalk. It won't show up completely on the glass (and will probably rub off) but you have magically infused that intention into the candle by the act of marking it.

Preparing your vigil candle is simple. Puncture 4 small holes into the wax in the sign of the cross and rub the MONEY DRAWING oil into the holes. Sprinkle a pinch of cinnamon powder across the surface of the wax. State your intention or place a petition under the candle and light. Tradition says that it is best to leave the candle burning continuously for the full seven days. If you do not feel comfortable leaving a burning candle lit while you are not at home, I always tell clients that I find it acceptable to simply thank the candle for its daily work before blowing it out then restate your intention each time you relight it. When the candle has finished, you can either bury the glass or, once again, thank the candle for its service and throw it away.

SPELLS OF CROSSING AND UNCROSSING

FOOT TRACK MAGIC CLEANSING –

this is based on an old Hoodoo rite for removing crossed conditions. It can be used to remove foot track magic (like hot foot) or for cleansing a home of the residue of foot track magic.

- What you will need:
- holy water
- ammonia
- powdered horseradish
- JINX BEGONE or SAINT CYPRIAN oil
- 3 straws from a broom
- plain water

The implementation is simple. Take about a half cup of ammonia and mix in a bucket with about 5 cups of water. Add a pinch of powdered horseradish, 3 straws from a broom, a dash of holy water, and about a capful of JINX BEGONE or CYPRIAN oil. Mix well. Take a rag or sponge and cleanse the four corners on the house (inside.) If you are concerned about the mixture spoiling carpeting (or anything else) then simply wipe down the baseboards in the four corners of the house. This does not mean the four corners of the person's room, but of the entire home. So, you will have to go from room to room to touch all four corners of the structure. When you have done this, take outside and dump the rest on the front porch. Feel free to pour more water on the porch to cleanse it. Now, the cleansing will be carried throughout the rest of your house whenever someone enters the front door.

UNCROSS AND REVERSE SPELL –

this is used when you are certain that someone has worked magic against you. It is even more powerful if you know who that person is. Uncross and Reverse isn't just about taking a jinx off of you – it's also about returning it back to the sender so that they can experience the same misery they wished upon you. Those who do not wish to perform works of revenge usually don't mind casting a reversing spell, as it sends nothing new out into the world – only reflecting back a work already created. For the spell below, if you do not know who cast a spell on you, just use a blank icon of a person, such as a profile silhouette.

- What you will need:
- Picture of person who cast hex or curse
- small mirror
- UNCROSS AND REVERSE oil
- hyssop herb
- 3 white spell candles
- 1 black spell candle
- bowl
- black cloth (about the size of a handkerchief)

First, you will need to take a ritual bath to remove the crossed conditions from you. Light two of the white candles and place one on each side of the bath tub. Take a bowl into the bathroom with you. Draw warm water in the tub, only about an ankle length deep. Drizzle a few capfuls of UNCROSS AND REVERSE oil into the bath water along with a teaspoon of dried hyssop. If you do not wish to have loose herbs in the tub, you can tie the hyssop into a coffee filter and submerge in water when you begin to draw the bath or steep the hyssop ahead of time (the same way you would make tea) and include in the bath water. Undress and step between the lit candles and into the tub. While standing, begin to gather the bath water into the bowl and slowly pour over your head while reciting the 23rd Psalm. Repeat this uncrossing baptism seven times. Gather up some of the bath water into the bowl and set aside. You may now step out of the tub, blow out the candles, and towel dry.

Take the picture of your enemy and draw X's over the eyes and several across the mouth. Anoint the picture with the UNCROSS AND REVERSE oil in the sign of the cross and place the photo under the mirror. Anoint the white candle with both the oil and your bath water. Anoint the black candle with only the oil. Place candles on either side of the mirror and light, praying for your condition to be removed and sent back to where it came from. Don't throw out the rest of the bath water yet. When the candles have finished burning, wrap the mirror and the picture of the person in the black cloth and hit with a hammer, breaking the glass. Tie up in a bundle. Throw the bath water toward the direction of the sunset (West) then drive the black bag off your property and bury it.

DOWN THE RIVER BOTTLE SPELL –

bottle spells thrown into running water are usually to send a person away from you – to a different location. If you live near a river, even better.

- What you will need:
- small bottle – between 2 and 4 ounces
- nails
- lemon juice
- CAST OUT AND BANISH oil

- picture of your target
- red peppers

If you do not have a picture of your target, write their name on a piece of paper seven times and write your petition over their name. If you do have a picture, write your petition over it stating exactly what you want to happen. Fold away from you as many times as possible and place in the bottle. Drop into the bottle the nails, peppers, and about 1/3 of the bottle of CAST OUT AND BANISH oil. Fill to the top with lemon juice, cap, and shake while restating your intention. Take to a place of running water, such as a river, and restate your intention again. Throw as hard as you can into the water and walk away without looking back.

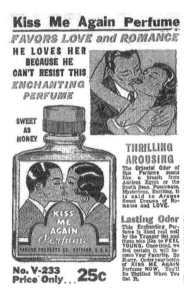

CONCOCTING YOUR OWN OIL BLENDS

Now that we have covered spells of love, protection, power, money, and dealing with baneful work, you can see how a spell is crafted using spiritual oils. This will help you create your own in the future. So far we've discovered that oils can be used on petition papers, to dress candles, inside bottle and jar spells, on people, on objects, and as an ingredient in creating other magical formulas.

We have also learned about many of the herbs, roots, flowers, and minerals used in the creation of oil blends and magic. If you choose to formulate your own oils, keep in mind that careful selection is a fundamental element to a good blend. In other words, don't go overboard. If you want a lover back, there is no need to use every ingredient listed that has love attracting properties. Many practitioners choose a magical number for their mystical concoctions. An oil, an herb bath, or a mojo bag often has a total of three, seven, nine, or thirteen ingredients. This isn't a hard and fast rule –merely a guideline. Trust the herbs and roots you have chosen for your particular blend and let them do their work. You may also substitute the inclusion of an herb or plant for its essential oil counterpart.

As an example of how to create your personal blends, we're going to formulate our own version of a CLEOPATRA OIL, using ingredients that are sexual, deal with love, and control. Tossing aside the concept of using a specific number of elements, we are going to use just five things:

- Calamus root (for control and domination)

- Queen Elizabeth root (for love, attraction, and feminine energy)

- Rose petals (for love, passion, and remembrance)

- Patchouli oil (for sex, satisfaction, and its aphrodisiac properties)

- Sandalwood oil (for passion, concentration, and the granting of wishes)

In a small bottle (about a ½ ounce in size), place a few pieces of calamus root, some pieces of Queen Elizabeth root, a pinch of rose petals, 10 drops of patchouli oil, and 5 drops of sandalwood oil. Fill the bottle the rest of the way with olive oil (or some other natural carrier oil) and shake well. At this point, you will have to turn to your personal practice to decide how you want to imbue the oil with magical intentions. Some may perform Reiki over the oils if they are of a healing nature. Others burn distinctive candles around the bottle. Someone else may simply pray over the blend. While the ingredients hold their own qualities of sympathetic magic already, the energy coming from you or your ritual will solidify the oil's overall and complete purpose.

EPILOGUE – ABOUT MAGIC AND MAGICAL PRODUCTS, A DISCLAIMER

I am often asked, "is magic real?" I always ask back, "are prayers real?" Neither can be seen or touched. All the products we create and the recipes we formulate are based on the historical uses of herbs, roots, flowers, barks, mineral, and zoological elements according to how they were implemented in spirituality and magic. It is up to you to use this historical knowledge to make your own informed decision about using magical products. Legally, all of the faith-based oils and other products we make must be sold as "curios" - for entertainment purposes. There can be no guarantee as to their magical properties. Can we guarantee they will work? I always remind clients that a doctor cannot guarantee he can cure you. A lawyer cannot guarantee you that he will win your court case. I can tell you that the more focus, involvement, and intention you place on the things most important to you usually creates movement. How you choose to create that movement and how you will act and react to it is in your own hands. Bright blessings.